Frederic W. Speirs

The Street Railway System of Philadelphia

It's History And Present Condition

Frederic W. Speirs

The Street Railway System of Philadelphia
It's History And Present Condition

ISBN/EAN: 9783744724982

Printed in Europe, USA, Canada, Australia, Japan

Cover: Foto ©ninafisch / pixelio.de

More available books at **www.hansebooks.com**

JOHNS HOPKINS UNIVERSITY STUDIES

IN

HISTORICAL AND POLITICAL SCIENCE

HERBERT B. ADAMS, Editor

History is past Politics and Politics are present History.—*Freeman*

FIFTEENTH SERIES

III–IV–V

THE STREET RAILWAY SYSTEM OF PHILADELPHIA
ITS HISTORY AND PRESENT CONDITION

By Frederic W. Speirs, Ph. D.

Professor of Economics and History, Drexel Institute, Philadelphia

BALTIMORE
The Johns Hopkins Press
PUBLISHED MONTHLY
March-April-May, 1897

CONTENTS.

CHAP.		PAGE.
	Introduction	7
I.	The Beginnings of Local Transportation in Philadelphia	9
II.	Episodes in the Early History of Street Railways: The Contest over Sunday Cars; The Admission of Negroes to Street Cars	18
III.	The Evolution of Monopoly	28
IV.	The Financial Aspects of the Railway System	37
V.	The Price of Franchise Privileges	53
VI.	Public Control	73
VII.	Municipal Ownership	83
VIII.	Corporate Influence in State and Municipal Government	92
IX.	The Railways and their Employees	100
	Bibliography	115
	Appendix	117

INTRODUCTION.

During the past few years the public mind has been awakening to a realization of the social and economic importance of the local transportation systems of great cities. Public opinion is beginning to demand that in the administration of such transportation systems the interests of the entire community rather than the promotion of private ends shall be regarded. Some of the European cities have assumed the direct management of their street railways, while American cities have attempted various plans of regulation and control of the corporations which conduct their service. These recent experiments to reduce the cost of service and improve its character have attracted much attention. But while there has been extended general discussion, there have been few comprehensive studies of particular systems in this country, and the discussion has thus suffered from the lack of exact knowledge regarding local conditions in American cities.

The present study is an attempt to make to the general discussion a contribution of fact regarding local transportation in one of the largest of our cities. It has been conceived as a strictly local study, and the temptation to indulge in comparisons and generalizations has been resisted as far as possible.

The railway system of Philadelphia presents many features of special interest to the student of the general problem. The city is spread over a large area, the municipal limits embracing 129 square miles, and the length of surface railway lines is thus greater than that of any other city in America, with the exception of Chicago. Philadelphia having adopted the "rail-bus" very early, the history of the system covers the entire period of railway development in this country. The experience of the city in the enforcement of the obligations imposed upon its companies for the purpose of securing compensation for franchise privileges is very instructive, and, unfortunately. not unique. The financial operations by which the values of railway stocks have been inflated until the present operating company is staggering under interest and lease charges amounting to 54 per cent. of gross receipts, are most interesting, although they do not possess the charm of novelty, being indeed quite typical of conditions in almost all large cities in this country. The process of monopolization is also typical, and therefore of more than local interest.

The writer is indebted to Professor Joseph French Johnson and Dr. L. S. Rowe, of the University of Pennsylvania, to Mr. Charles Richardson, of the Municipal League, and to Mr. Joseph H. Patterson, of the editorial staff of the *Evening Telegraph*, who have read the proof and offered valued suggestions. He is also indebted to Mr. Talcott Williams, of the *Philadelphia Press*, who with characteristic generosity lightened the burden of consulting newspaper files by extending the privilege of the use of his large collection of clippings.

THE STREET RAILWAY SYSTEM OF PHILADELPHIA.
ITS HISTORY AND PRESENT CONDITION.

CHAPTER I.

THE BEGINNINGS OF LOCAL TRANSPORTATION IN PHILADELPHIA.

The history of local transportation in Philadelphia begins in 1831. At this time the municipal limits, which had not been enlarged since the grant of the original charter by Penn, in 1701, embraced about two square miles, containing a population of about 81,000. But by 1831 the urban population had greatly outgrown the limits of the original city, and Philadelphia was surrounded by a fringe of boroughs, townships and incorporated districts, independent governmentally, but, in conjunction with the city, constituting physically a single urban district of about 175,000 inhabitants.

The inauguration of a system of local transportation was heralded by the following newspaper advertisement which appeared in December, 1831: "James Boxall having been requested by several gentlemen to run an hourly stagecoach for the accommodation of the inhabitants of Chestnut Street, to and from the lower part of the city, begs to inform the citizens generally that he has provided a superior new coach, harness and good horses for that purpose. Comfort, warmth and neatness have in every respect been carefully studied. This conveyance will start from Schuylkill-seventh and Chestnut Streets every morning (Sundays excepted) at 8.30 o'clock, every hour until 4.30 in the afternoon, down Chestnut Street to the Merchant's Coffee House in Second

Street; and return from the Coffee House at 9 o'clock, and every hour until 5 in the evening. This accommodation will be conducted and driven solely by the proprietor, who hopes to merit patronage and support. Fare each way, 10 cents; or tickets may be had of the proprietor at twelve for one dollar."

The Boxall Hourly Stage Coach proved profitable, and in 1833 an omnibus line was established, running at right angles with the original line the extreme length of the city, from the Navy Yard to Kensington, by way of Second Street. Omnibuses ran hourly on this route, conveying passengers for 12½ cents. The success of these early ventures led to the rapid multiplication of omnibus lines, and soon ponderous vehicles were rattling over the cobblestones and floundering through the mud-holes of Philadelphia's main thoroughfares in such numbers as to give very satisfactory transportation facilities to the rapidly growing city.

Many of these lines were supported by subscription, each subscriber buying an annual ticket at a price which amounted to the very reasonable fare of a penny a ride for those who rode regularly four times a day. Non-subscribers paid ten cents or twelve and one-half cents for each ride in the early days, but later competition reduced the single fare as low as three cents on some of the shorter lines.

The omnibuses held the transportation field unchallenged and played a most important part in the development of the city for about twenty-five years, and then, in 1858, coming into competition with the street cars, they were forced out of use by their more rapid and comfortable rivals. The speedy disappearance of the omnibuses on the advent of street railways is indicated by the license returns as given in the reports of the City Controllers. In 1855 the municipal Councils had passed an ordinance exacting an annual license fee of fifteen dollars for each omnibus regularly running on the streets. In 1857, the year before the first street railway was opened, the amount of these fees indicates that 322 omnibuses were in service; in 1858 the number had fallen to 222;

in 1859 there were only 56 of the omnibuses in use; while in 1864 the total return from the omnibus tax was $15, witnessing that one lone survivor was offering the public the privilege of jolting over the cobbles in the good old-fashioned way. The withdrawal of the omnibuses was facilitated by the charter provision of the newly incorporated railway companies, which forced them to purchase at a fair valuation the equipment of the omnibus companies.

Meantime John Stephenson had been working on his idea of an omnibus running on rails laid in the street. As far back as 1832 he had built a " rail-bus," accommodating thirty persons in three compartments, with seats on top for additional passengers. This had been placed on the New York and Harlem Railroad. The innovation does not seem to have been well received, and for twenty years the idea lay dormant. Then it was revived, and capitalists sought from the legislatures of Massachusetts, New York and Pennsylvania authority to construct " horse-power railways," as they were then termed. Philadelphia, being a large city spread over a considerable area, was naturally one of the most promising fields for investment in the new enterprise.

As early as 1855 the Councils appointed a " Special Committee on City Passenger Railroads." This committee sought an opinion on the desirability of these roads from Mr. Strickland Kneass, Chief Engineer and Surveyor. In a report dated October 12, 1855, he pointed out the great advantages of the proposed railways in comparison with the omnibus system and gave the committee detailed information with reference to the engineering questions involved.

On June 9, 1857, the Philadelphia and Delaware River R. R. Company, operating a steam road, secured from the General Assembly of Pennsylvania a supplement to its charter, authorizing the construction of a street railway on Fifth and Sixth Streets, to be operated by horses, and on January 20, 1858, the first street car line in Philadelphia was opened to the public.

This first railway was built in face of wide-spread opposition. Street railways had been for some time in successful operation in New York and Boston before the first Philadelphia road was begun, but the advantages of the "rail bus," which the experiments in these cities had placed beyond question, do not seem to have deeply impressed the citizens of Philadelphia.

On February 23, 1857, while the charter of the first street railway was pending, there was presented to the General Assembly "An Address and Remonstrance against the Fifth and Sixth Streets Railway," signed by twelve hundred residents along the proposed line. Several of the newspapers protested against the introduction of the railways, and a considerable number of the most prominent and influential citizens supported the opposition. Elaborate arguments against the system were printed in pamphlet form and circulated by zealous opponents. The principal objections as reflected by the pamphlets and newspapers of the day may be summarized as follows, stripped of their extravagant verbiage:

(1) That the proposed railways were a mischievous speculation, aiming at monopoly of transportation along the great lines of travel.

(2) That the rapidly moving cars could not be readily stopped and would thus be exceedingly dangerous to life and limb.[1]

(3) That the cars would disturb the repose of the streets through which they passed and make city life intolerable by the increase of noise.

(4) That on account of the danger of the railways and of

---

[1] "It is perhaps scarcely worth while to allude to the fact that in New York they kill one person each week on city railroads and mangle three or four upon an average in the same space of time. .... Human life is really of little value now-a-days, and the general opinion among railway corporators is that people that get in the way of the cars 'ought to get killed.' "—*Sunday Dispatch*, June 21, 1857.

See table of accidents on passenger railways in appendix, page 123.

the noise, property along the lines would be heavily depreciated.

(5) That the streets were already overcrowded, and the introduction of railways would increase the congestion of traffic.

(6) That the rails would ruin the streets for the use of carriages and wagons.

The advocates of the new system took the ground that the opposition to railways was but a new phase of an old antagonism to progress. A pamphlet published by railway promoters begins: "That conspicuous ascendancy over all cities of America which, at one period, was the incontestable prerogative of Philadelphia, is gradually but palpably passing away. Her financial, commercial and political supremacy are already gone. A palsy seems to have stricken her. .... Her policy now is but a reflex of what it was some forty years ago—the era at which her relative retrogression visibly began. Four or five years of ferocious resistance were then opposed to the introduction of hydrant water. .... A similar scene transpired upon the introduction of gas. Five or six years were spent in the most furious agitation before our intolerable fogyism could be dissipated. .... Last, but not least, in the same category, come city railways."

Much vigorous Anglo-Saxon was used on both sides and the fight waxed warm. It was quite generally believed that corrupt influences were at work in the General Assembly to secure the supplementary charter authorizing the construction of the railway, and many who looked with favor on the railway system felt constrained to oppose the grant of privileges to the Philadelphia and Delaware River R. R. Company. The protest was unavailing, and the charter for the Fifth and Sixth Streets line was granted, the passage of the act being announced editorially by one of the local papers under the heading "Sold and Delivered." Of the charter, the editorial says: "Conceived in wickedness and brought forth in infamy, it is a monument of disgrace to a Pennsylvania Legislature."

Once in operation, the first railway proved an immediate financial success. This success inspired numerous applications to the General Assembly for charters for other lines. The convenience of the new system as exemplified by the Fifth and Sixth Streets railway caused many to forsake the ranks of the opposition, but the objectors were still numerous and active. The opponents of the Second and Third Streets Passenger Railway Company, chartered in 1858, invoked the aid of the courts in their struggle against it. They asked for an injunction to prevent the construction of the road, on the ground that the proposed railway would be a public nuisance.[1] The injunction was denied, the Court saying that while a railway may "occasion loss or inconvenience, it may depreciate the value of property and render its enjoyment incommodious and almost impossible, yet this is *damnum absque injuria.*" After this decision the remonstrants abandoned hope of relief from the courts.

In 1858 a charter was secured authorizing a railway company to occupy two of the most important business and residence streets in the city, Chestnut and Walnut Streets. A perfect storm of protest was aroused by the threatened invasion of these sacred precincts. Since the General Assembly had already granted the charter, the remonstrants turned to Councils, praying that the consent of the representative body of the city, which was requisite for the construction of the road, should be refused. The seriousness of the protest is disclosed by a petition submitted to Councils, in which it is shown that the owners of 16,660 feet of taxable real estate frontage on the streets involved, out of a total frontage of 30,327 feet, oppose the railway. An interesting side light is thrown on the methods of street railway promoters in those early days by the statement in a pamphlet[2] published by the remonstrants, that when the

---

[1] Faust et al. vs. Passenger Railway Co., 3 Phila. Reports, 164.

[2] Objections to the Approval by City Councils of the Charter of the Central Pass. Ry. Co. By "Philadelphian." August 21, 1858.

petitions in favor of the railway were analyzed it was found that 216 names on the petitions were not in the city directory of that year, 290 signers lived at a distance from the streets named, and only 42 of the petitioners were persons directly interested in the streets which the railway wished to occupy.

The arguments against the grant to the railway company are interesting. The opposition, in this case, does not appeal to the prejudice and blind conservatism brought into play earlier, but rests its case on three points, the last two of which might be seriously urged to-day under similar conditions. These points are: (1) Injury to property-holders along the line; (2) Indefinite powers granted to the company by the charter; (3) Inadequate return to the city for the valuable privileges asked. The argument on the first point aims to show that the property-holders on Chestnut and Walnut Streets will sustain through the construction of the road an injury estimated at $1,500,000. In the second place, the charter is shown to convey very large powers to the company, with inadequate control by the municipality. In the third place, the remonstrants proceed to a consideration which is most interesting in the light of later developments. The terms of the proposed grant called for the payment to the city of a license fee of fifty dollars for each car used on the line, and also required the company to keep in repair the streets occupied by its tracks. " What, then, should be the price paid by the company for such important privileges and concessions to them? It will not be gravely maintained that the price stipulated in the charter is anything but a mockery." It is then urged that if the streets are to be given to the company, Councils should prescribe an " equitable bonus " for privileges granted, and in addition require shares of capital stock to be sold at auction and the premium on sales to be paid into the city treasury. The railway promoters had made much of the large benefit which the city was to receive from their enterprises, and in many cases had posed as unselfish devotees of the public weal.

The opponents remark that in some quarters there has been manifested a disposition to question the sincerity of this devotion to the public good, and even to insinuate that the zeal of the railway promoters was due in large measure to expectations of excessive private profit. The remonstrants thus demand from Councils provision for an adequate return to the city for the valuable privileges requested, urging that the railway promoters who claim to have the public interest at heart cannot consistently oppose an ordinance safeguarding that interest.

The clever and forcible protest did not avail. Chestnut and Walnut Streets were given over to the Central Passenger Railway Company without the imposition of the conditions requested. It was freely charged at the time that the railway company had opposed to the reasoning of the remonstrants the less admirable but more effective argument of stock distribution among the Councilmen, and unfortunately the experience of Philadelphians with their municipal Councils has been such as to make it easy for the average citizen to credit the charge.

Meantime the construction of the lines was being rapidly pushed. Two companies had been incorporated in 1857, ten were chartered in 1858, and six more in 1859. Thus within two years from the grant of the first charter, eighteen railway companies held franchises in Philadelphia. The excessive liberality of the General Assembly in the matter of grants to street railway promoters was viewed with alarm even by the most progressive citizens, who had warmly welcomed the first railways. But the enlightened protest against the multiplication of companies was futile. An attack of what was termed by the men of the time "passenger railway insanity" had seized the investors, and with a complacent State legislature to grant charters and a not over-scrupulous municipal legislature to approve the grants, the construction of roads went on with great rapidity. The great panic of 1857 had swept the country, leaving financial ruin behind, but there was no lack of money to build the railways, and most of those authorized were promptly put in operation.

By August, 1858, seven roads were under contract, the total length being about fifty miles. On five of these roads in operation late in 1858, the total number of passengers carried daily was estimated at 46,000. The new roads not only absorbed all the business of the old omnibuses and drove them from the field, but the improved facilities greatly stimulated travel. We are told, for example, in 1858, that on the Philadelphia and Darby Railway, running through a suburban district, "five cars are insufficient to accommodate the permanent travel originally performed by one omnibus."

The new transportation system rapidly conquered public favor. Even the ultra-conservatives, who threatened to sell their property and leave the city if the dreaded railway were allowed to invade the peaceful streets of Philadelphia, remained to ride in the new conveyances, and learned with pleasure that even the dangerous horse car, whose wild rush through their streets they had anticipated with alarm, might in the proper environment be regulated to a rate of progress entirely safe and quite in keeping with the requirements of a city which had a reputation for sobriety and moderation to maintain. In January, 1859, Mayor Henry was able to say in his message to Councils: "Perhaps no public improvement ever occasioned more contrariety of opinion than the occupation by the passenger railway system of the streets of this city, and perhaps none has ever promised more general benefit to the community."

CHAPTER II.

Episodes in the Early History of Street Railways—The Contest over Sunday Cars—The Admission of Negroes to Street Cars.

The Contest over Sunday Cars.

The community had hardly settled down to a cheerful acceptance of the new system of transportation when it was aroused to renewed controversy over the passenger railways. Two lines announced their intention of running cars on Sunday, beginning July 10, 1859.

Philadelphia had from the beginning most rigorously observed the day of rest. All public conveyances were stopped on that day. A law of 1798 had even authorized churches to stretch chains across the streets in front of their houses of worship, in order that the passage of carriages should not disturb the service. In 1853 an attempt to run omnibuses on Sunday in Pittsburg had resulted in a decision of the Supreme Court[1] that such action was in violation of law.[2]

Anticipating opposition to Sunday travel from the conservative religious element in the community, the management of the Ridge Avenue and Manayunk Company diplomatically added to their newspaper announcement of Sunday cars: "This arrangement will enable persons residing temporarily in the country to attend their usual places of worship in the city."

---

[1] Commonwealth vs. Johnson, 22 Pa. State Reports, 102.

[2] The statute quoted in this and subsequent cases dated back to 1794. It provided, "If any person shall do or perform any worldly employment or business whatsoever on the Lord's Day, commonly called Sunday (works of necessity and charity only excepted) . . . every such person so offending shall, for every such offense, forfeit and pay four dollars . . . or suffer six days imprisonment."

But the diplomacy was unavailing. A storm of protest greeted the operation of the roads on the first Sunday. The citizens opposed to Sunday cars appealed to Mayor Henry, and he undertook to convey their protest to the companies in his official capacity. The directors of the companies involved refused to accede to the wishes of the mayor and the citizens whom he represented, but agreed to compromise by refraining from starting the cars until one o'clock in the afternoon, by removing bells, and by ordering drivers to walk their horses past all places of public worship and to carefully avoid all unnecessary noise.

On July 17, the second Sunday, the driver of the first car out of the barn was immediately arrested, charged with breach of the peace. On habeas corpus proceedings, Judge Thompson, of the Supreme Bench, held the driver for trial, declaring that in his opinion the operation of cars on Sunday was in violation of the statute of 1794, already cited.[1] The judge said significantly: "This city has for one hundred and fifty years obeyed the law faithfully in its observance of the Sabbath, and it is not perceptible wherein either its prosperity or character has suffered." On trial in Quarter Sessions the driver was released on the ground that since he had been arrested as soon as his car left the barn, no breach of the peace had actually occurred.

Meantime the discussion raged hotly in the columns of the newspapers and in mass-meetings. Large public meetings of the opponents of Sunday travel were held on Tuesday, July 12, and on Friday, July 15, 1859. The advocates of Sunday cars gathered in mass-meeting in Independence Square on July 21 and July 30, and listened with enthusiasm to vehement speeches on individual liberty. At the meeting of July 30, a Committee of Ninety-Six was appointed to secure for the people the right of Sunday travel.

Parts of the discussion which have been preserved in the columns of the newspapers of the day are highly diverting. In a letter entitled "The Origin of Sunday and the Char-

---

[1] Commonwealth vs. Jeandelle, 2 Grant's Cases, 506.

acter of Constantine, its Founder," a correspondent of the *Sunday Dispatch* gravely argues for the right of the people to street car service on Sunday on the ground that Constantine, the originator of the observance of Sunday, foully murdered two brothers-in-law, a nephew, and an intimate friend, in addition to boiling his wife to death, and therefore Constantine and his institution of Sunday were not entitled to the respect of the good people of Philadelphia.

The opposition to Sunday travel scored a triumph on October 18, 1859, when the stockholders of the road which had led the movement for Sunday railway service, by unanimous vote, decreed that thereafter traffic on their line should be suspended on the first day of the week.

However, during the following year the Frankford and Southwark Company for a time ran cars from their Frankford terminus a considerable distance toward the centre of the city, and then made connections with omnibuses which conveyed their passengers the rest of the distance. In a few other instances the railways ran cars on Sunday, but there was no attempt to establish regular travel on that day for several years.

Sunday cars were already running in Boston, New York, Baltimore, Washington, St. Louis, Chicago and several other cities, when late in 1865 the Union Passenger Railway Company determined to operate its road on the first day of the week. To forestall an attempt to stop the cars the Company resorted to the expedient of securing from the United States government a contract to carry the mails. The ingenious device of running the cars on Sunday under the protection of the Federal authorities aggravated the indignation of the opponents of Sunday travel, and the community was mightily stirred by the ensuing discussion.

A bill in equity for injunction against the Union Company to prevent the running of Sunday cars was finally filed, under the claim that the operation of the railways on that day involved injury to the plaintiffs in their rights of property in their houses and their church pews. In December,

1866, Judge Strong, in Nisi Prius, granted the preliminary injunction, and the case went to the Supreme Court. The decision in Nisi Prius was not unexpected, since Judge Strong had presided at one of the church meetings called to protest against Sunday cars.

Meantime the aid of the General Assembly of Pennsylvania had been invoked by those who wished to use the cars on Sunday, and in the spring of 1866 a bill had been introduced providing that the question should be submitted to the vote of the people of Philadelphia. The sentiment of the Senate is sufficiently indicated by its reference of the bill to the "Committee on Vice and Immorality." The committee failed to report the bill. The measure was also defeated in the House.

In the session of 1867 another attempt was made to secure legislative sanction for Sunday cars. The bill was defeated by a close vote in the Senate, all the Philadelphia senators voting for it. The apprehension of the extreme conservatives with reference to the effects of Sunday cars is voiced by a speech made while the bill was under consideration in the House, by a country member, M. B. Lowry. He said: "This bill will require you to double your police force on the Sabbath, it will throng your mayor's court on Monday morning, it will fill your almshouses with starving children during the week, it will decrease your Sabbath schools and increase your prisons, it will open the road to vice and fill the highways with its votaries."

But although such argument availed with the country members of the Legislature, the triumph of the advocates of Sunday cars was close at hand. The injunction case, already mentioned, was considered by the Supreme Court in November, 1867. Mr. Sparhawk and the others contended that the operation of the railways on Sunday depreciated the value of their houses and their pews. Their statement says: "The effect of the disturbing influences complained of is shown as well in the cases of the appellees, who are residents and owners of property, some of whom have actually been compelled to abandon the use of their front rooms on Sunday and retire to other parts of their dwellings, in order that they might engage in such devotional exercises as they had been accustomed to, with their families, on that day." From the standpoint of disturbance of public worship, Rev. John W. Mears presents the case of the opposition to Sunday cars in the following testimony: "It was necessary for me to make an unusual effort to keep up the train of thought, to make my voice audible as it should be. To be thus compelled, in a regular Sunday service, to pray against or in rivalry with outside noises, I consider a grievous annoyance, and one against which I, as a worshipper of God and leader of the devotions of others, should be protected in a professedly Christian commonwealth."

In reply to the statements of the appellees, the railway company averred that in running their cars on Sunday they were performing an act of necessity and, moreover, of charity, since they were promoting the cause of true religion as well as the health of the city by assisting people to go to church and to breathe fresh air.

The Court declared that injunction was not the proper remedy, since the action complained of was not an injury which should be dealt with by equity process. The case came under the statute of 1794, providing a fine as the penalty of infraction. Permanent injunction was therefore denied. Justice Read, concurring with his colleagues, went much further than the majority of the Court. In a learned opinion fairly bristling with passages of Scripture, and quoting Luther, Calvin, Jeremy Taylor, William Penn, Bishop White, Pliny's letter to Trajan, the Edict of Constantine, Barclay's Apology, and several other notable men and documents, he maintained that the running of the cars on Sunday was not in violation of existing statutes. After an exhaustive review of Sunday legislation, he concludes: "I place my opinion, therefore, of the entire legality of running passenger cars on Sunday on the same footing with

Sunday trains of steam railroads, as being clearly within the exceptions both of necessity and charity."[1]

Injunction having been refused, the opponents of Sunday travel did not avail themselves of the suggestion of the Court that the companies might be punished by fine under the act of 1794, and no further attempt was made to stop the cars. On November 9, 1867, the Union Company announced that under the decision of the Supreme Court the regular Sunday trips would be resumed. The other lines speedily followed the example of the Union Company, and thus the controversy was closed.

The Admission of Negroes to Street Cars.

While the citizens of Philadelphia were contending over the question of Sunday cars, another issue appeared which ranged the people of the city on new controversial lines in the street car arena. This was the question of the admission of the colored people to the street cars.[2]

From the outset the negroes had been excluded from the street cars, or, as a measure of grace, allowed to stand on the front platform. The legal right of the companies to exclude the colored people had been affirmed by the courts. In 1861 an action for damages was brought by a colored man against a conductor who had ejected him from a car, and the court had found for the defendant. In this case Judge Hare said: "In the belief, then, that the regulation (excluding negroes) now before us is a wise one, or, if not wise, will work its own cure best when least molested, we enter judgment for the defendant."[3]

---

[1] Sparhawk et al. vs. Union Passenger Railway Co., 54 Pa. State Reports, 401.

[2] For a Northern city, Philadelphia contained in 1860 a large negro population. The national census of that year shows that the colored people made up one seventy-seventh of the population of Boston, one sixty-third of the population of New York City, and one twenty-fourth of the population of Philadelphia.

[3] Goines vs. McCandless, 4 Philadelphia Reports, 255.

There seems to have been no general disposition to question the wisdom or justice of this decision until the persistent but unavailing arguments of the friends of legal equality for the negro were reinforced by the unanswerable logic of the Civil War. Then there was issued a call for a public meeting on January 13, 1865, to take measures to secure for the colored people the right to use the street cars. This call was signed by about seventy prominent citizens, among them Henry C. Carey, the eminent economist, Phillips Brooks, T. DeWitt Talmage, Jay Cooke, and other notable men of more strictly local reputation. At this meeting on January 13 an influential committee of thirty was appointed to secure the opening of the street cars to the colored people of Philadelphia. The sentiment of the meeting was expressed by a series of forcible resolutions asserting the right of the colored people to share the benefits of railway transportation.[1]

The committee appointed by this meeting addressed the presidents of the nineteen street railway companies, requesting them to rescind the regulation excluding colored people from the cars. The companies replied that they could not

---

[1] "*Resolved*, That in the words of our venerable and respected townsman, whose name leads the call for this meeting, we are 'opposed to the exclusion of respectable persons from our passenger railway cars on the ground of complexion.'

Resolved, That we have heard with shame and sorrow the statements that decent women of color have been forced to walk long distances, or to accept standing positions on the front platforms of cars, exposed to the inclemency of the weather, while visiting, at our military hospitals, their relatives who have been wounded in the defense of their country.

Resolved, That we respectfully request the presidents and directors of our city passenger railways to withdraw from their list of regulations this rule of exclusion which deprives our people of color of their rights, and is in direct opposition to the recent decisions of our courts of justice.

Resolved, That in view of these recent decisions, the rights of our colored population in respect to the cars are without reserve; and to confine them to the use of special cars bearing aloft the degrading labels of caste, and running at long intervals, is a simple substitution of one act of injustice for another, and is as much in violation of their rights as the rule of total exclusion."

admit colored people in opposition to the wishes of their patrons, and offered the somewhat remarkable proposition that the matter be determined by a car vote of their patrons. The committee remonstrated in vain against the folly of this plan, and the car vote was taken on January 30 and 31, 1865. After two days of "tumultuous balloting," with the conductors as ballot receivers and judges, an overwhelming majority against admission was reported.

The Frankford and Southwark Company tried the experiment of admitting colored people for one month, and then abandoned the policy. The men employed in the Navy Yard and the women who were working there on government clothing were patrons of this line, and their strenuous opposition did much to defeat the experiment. On a few lines separate cars were run at long intervals for the accommodation of the colored people, but the results were not satisfactory to the companies nor to the colored population.

After their vain appeal to the railway companies the committee next turned to Mayor Henry, requesting him to prevent the police from assisting conductors in ejecting colored people. He declined to act, frankly stating his personal prejudice against riding with negroes.

A bill was, meantime, prepared and introduced in the General Assembly during the session of 1865, providing that railway companies should not be allowed to make color discriminations. It passed the Senate, but the House committee refused to report it.

While the committee working for the colored people had been engaged in trying to secure concessions from the railway companies and legislation from the General Assembly, they had also been active in an attempt to secure a judicial interpretation of existing law in favor of admission. They tried to prosecute criminally conductors who had ejected negroes from their cars, but although nine cases were brought to the attention of grand juries, these bodies refused to indict. The committee had more success with civil cases, and damages were secured in several instances.

The most notable was the case of a colored woman who was violently thrust from a car while on her way home late at night from her 'church, where she had been engaged in providing comforts for wounded soldiers. Judge Allison charged the jury that common carriers cannot make color discriminations, and a verdict was rendered under his instruction assessing damages at fifty dollars. In his charge he said: " The logic of events of the past four years has in many respects cleared our vision and corrected our judgment; and no proposition has been more clearly wrought out by them than that the men who have been deemed worthy to become the defenders of the country, to wear the uniform of the soldier of the United States, should not be denied the rights common to humanity."[1]

A decision of the Supreme Court was sought, since the companies did not change their regulations after the adverse decisions of the lower courts, but meantime the question had assumed a political aspect, and many of the very members of the General Assembly who refused in 1865 to report a bill for admission now became most zealous advocates of the rights of the colored people. The explanation of the sudden change of heart lies in the fact that the negro was thenceforward to be reckoned with as a political force, since he was to be armed with the ballot. So on March 22, 1867, an act was passed with little opposition admitting the colored people to the street cars on equal terms with their white neighbors.

The exclusion had been complete until the passage of the act, and the admission was attended by some rioting, but in a short time the patrons of the cars accepted their new fellow travellers with perfect good nature.

It is notable that the committee which conducted this admirable campaign for the recognition of the rights of the colored people received little support from the press and the pulpit. Of seven daily newspapers, only two, the *Press* and

---

[1] Derry vs. Lowry, 6 Philadelphia Reports, 30.

the *Bulletin*, lent their aid to the movement in behalf of the negroes. But the silence of the pulpit is more noteworthy than that of the press. Most of the clergy ignored the question, although it was urged upon their attention while they were vigorously agitating against Sunday cars. Even when a brother minister, Rev. Mr. Allston, rector of St. Thomas Colored Episcopal Church, was forcibly expelled from a Lombard and South Streets car, the clergy uttered no protest. A pamphlet published in 1866 asserts that up to that time only three white clergymen had referred to the question in their pulpits.[1]

The committee that had done such excellent service in behalf of the colored people made a report in 1867,[2] which closes with the following survey of the situation immediately after the admission of the negroes to the cars: " The conduct of our colored friends in the use of their newly acquired right has been all but faultless. With an instinctive sense of propriety, which, it is feared, would be looked for in vain in any other race under like circumstances, they now enter the cars, not with an air of exultation at having gained a disputed point, but as if the point had never been disputed. It is also remarked that they resort to the cars sparingly, and, when not in clean clothes, voluntarily take their old places on the front platform. The most offensive occupants of seats—the drunken, the profane, the tobacco-chewing, the unwashed and selfish—are still of color other than black or brown. . . . Many men and women who, within the last few weeks, have found themselves seated for the first time beside decent and well-behaved colored people, and this without harm or annoyance from the so much dreaded contact, have also found stirring within their hearts, in consequence, a new influx of Christian charity."

---

[1] Why Colored People in Phila. are excluded from Street Cars. 1866.

[2] Report of Committee appointed for the Purpose of Securing to Colored Persons in Philadelphia the Right to the Use of Street Cars.

CHAPTER III.

THE EVOLUTION OF MONOPOLY IN STREET RAILWAY SERVICE.

Economic law in urban transportation was unconsciously defied by the General Assembly of Pennsylvania when the street railway system was established. The General Assembly said, "Let there be competition," where economic law says no real and permanent competition can exist. In the almost complete monopolization of her street car service, accomplished in the fall of 1895, Philadelphia has witnessed the vindication of the law that is above that of legislative assemblies.

Viewed from the standpoint of the evolution of monopoly, the history of the street railways of Philadelphia is most instructive and quite typical. In the beginning, street railway privileges were obtained by a large number of independent companies. During the period from 1857 to 1874 thirty-nine separate passenger railway companies were given charter right to operate street railways in the city of Philadelphia. Most of these companies constructed their lines, and for several years maintained an independent existence. The General Assembly defended the creation of this large number of railway corporations on the ground that the establishment of several independent lines would lead to healthful competition which would safeguard public interests. In several cases we find the following preamble in legislative grants: "Whereas, The interests of the public demand that no corporation should have the monopoly of carrying passengers over the streets of a city between points which require the advantages of competition," etc.

We note, however, that at the very beginning the companies found it advantageous to enter into alliance for the regulation of competition. This alliance took the form of a Board of Presidents of City Passenger Railway Companies, which was organized May 24, 1859, ten separate companies being represented at the outset. As new companies went into operation their presidents were added to the Board. The Board remained in active existence until the formation of the Union Traction Company in 1895, when the unity of policy which it had been created to maintain, was assured by a more effective agency, a complete legal monopoly.

Meantime the Board had been a most important factor in railway management. The principal matters with which it dealt were the regulation of fares and the arrangement of transfers, and its control in these respects was most effective. Philadelphia never had a rate war on her street railways. With few and unimportant exceptions, the numerous companies maintained a uniform rate of fare throughout their entire history. Whenever the fare was raised or lowered the change was announced as the action of the Board of Presidents. It appears that no pretense was ever made of independent action in this important matter. There was, of course, no legal control exercised by this extra-legal body. The action was always represented as the result of unanimous agreement on the part of the presidents of the several roads. But that there was a hand of iron in the glove of velvet appears from the experience of the West Philadelphia Company when early in its history it undertook to sell twenty-five tickets for one dollar, while the fare on the other roads was five cents. The president of the road which thus cut rates was requested to withdraw from the Board, and was only admitted again to its privileges after the restoration of the standard rate and an ample apology.

The practical effect of the existence of such a body was early recognized, and when the fare was raised first from five to six cents and later from six to seven cents the public protested vigorously against "the illegal attempt to stifle that healthful competition which the General Assembly intended to establish." The action of the Board was even denounced as conspiracy punishable under the common law.

It is thus apparent that the multiplicity of companies failed from the outset to secure that effective competition in price of service which was urged as the justification for the grant of the numerous franchises. The real result was the evil of a monopoly price without the advantage of the economy of operation which direct monopoly management would have made possible.

Within a few years after the inauguration of the street railway system, the natural economic law, which was to take nearly forty years to do its perfect work, began to make its influence felt, although the results in the beginning were not of great importance. The first instance of consolidation occurred in 1864, and during the next decade four companies were merged with stronger organizations and three were leased.

In 1876 the street railways of Philadelphia were in the hands of seventeen separate companies, operating their lines theoretically in entire independence, but in fact under the coöperative control of the Board of Railway Presidents. The total length of lines was about 289 miles. Of this mileage the largest amount owned by a single company was 41. The five companies possessing the longest lines were as follows:

Union	41	miles.
Second and Third Sts.	37	"
Germantown	31	"
Hestonville, Mantua & Fairmount	20	"
West Philadelphia	19	"

The total number of passengers carried was about 117,000,000,[1] the largest number carried by any one company being 15,008,950. From the standpoint of the number of

---

[1] This was the year of the Centennial Exposition and the number of passengers for this year was consequently much larger than usual.

passengers carried, the five most important companies were:

West Philadelphia	15,008,950
Philadelphia City	13,736,705
Germantown	13,338,672
Union	11,392,326
Hestonville, Mantua & Fairmount	9,634,689

Shortly after this, about 1880, the current began to set strong toward monopoly. In that year the Union Passenger Railway Company laid the foundation for the first extensive system of lines by its lease of the Continental Passenger Railway Company, which had, in 1879, effected a lease of the Seventeenth & Nineteenth Sts. Passenger Railway Company. A year later, in 1881, a second important system was created by the lease of two roads[1] by a hitherto unimportant company, the People's Passenger Railway Company, originally possessing but six miles of track. The figures for 1883 show that a single company, the Union, controlled 70 miles, and a second, the People's, 44 miles, out of a total mileage of 298. The Union Company carried 22,741,228 passengers, and the People's system 20,053,497, out of a total of about 110,000,000 carried by all the lines.

Thus far had consolidation of interests progressed when a new and important impulse to monopolization was given by the formation of the Philadelphia Traction Company, incorporated in 1883. This company was formed not with the intention of building a new street railway, but for the purpose of getting control of the existing railways by lease or purchase. Its projectors, Mr. P. A. B. Widener and Mr. W. L. Elkins, have since gained national reputation as street railway organizers, and the Widener-Elkins syndicate, as it is called, has controlled street railway systems in Chicago, New York, Pittsburg, and other large cities.

---

[1] Germantown Pass. Ry. Co. and Green & Coates Sts. Pass. Ry. Co.

These gentlemen and their associates appreciated the enormous profits which street railway enterprise could be made to yield, and planned a consolidation by lease of the original companies.

In fulfillment of its purpose, the Philadelphia Traction Company began at once to weld the railways of the city into a system far-reaching and powerful. In 1884 the Union system, already described, and another most important railway, the West Philadelphia, were leased. The Union Company controlled by lease the lines of the Continental Company, which in turn had leased, in 1879, the Seventeenth & Nineteenth Sts. road, the latter company owning one-half of the stock of the Empire Company; while the West Philadelphia Company held a lease of the Philadelphia City Railway, which at the time was operating the Philadelphia & Darby road. Thus the Philadelphia Traction Company, at the close of 1884, represented the consolidated interests of six of the original companies and held a half interest in a seventh. In 1885 it operated 116 miles of track out of a total mileage of about 320, and carried 42,039,344 passengers out of a total of about 117,170,000 carried by all the companies during that year. In other words, in 1885, the Traction Company controlled about 36 per cent. of the mileage of city railways and carried nearly 36 per cent. of all the passengers.

But the Philadelphia Traction Company was not satisfied with the powers that it possessed under the ordinary corporate organization, and so, using the potent political influence which it had acquired, it forced, in 1887, the passage of an act providing for the special incorporation of motor power companies and giving them large powers.[1] November 28, 1888, the Company was reorganized under this act, thus specifically acquiring the power "to invest its funds in the purchase of shares of stock and bonds of any corporation whose works, railway motors or other prop-

---

[1] Act of March 22, 1887.

erty are leased, operated or constructed by it," and "to lease the property and franchises of passenger railway companies which they may desire to operate, and to operate said railways." Under this form of incorporation the two traction companies which have recently united with the Philadelphia Traction Company to form the Union Traction Company were also organized.

The passage by the General Assembly of this act incorporating motor companies aroused intense popular opposition, and a great mass-meeting was held on March 1, 1887, to protest against its signature by the Governor, and incidentally to demand the reduction of fares from six cents to five cents. At that meeting Mr. Wayne MacVeagh made an interesting prophecy which was fulfilled eight years later. "You may rest assured your street railway system is destined very soon to be an absolute monopoly. You cannot stop it. Legislators cannot stop it. The only question remaining is whether the monopoly shall be owned by the Traction Company or the whole body of the good people of Philadelphia."

For six years after the formation of the Philadelphia Traction Company system there was little advance toward monopolization. Then, in 1890 and 1891, the Traction Company acquired two important lines, those of the Catherine and Bainbridge Sts. Company and the Philadelphia & Gray's Ferry Company. In 1892 the Traction system was practically completed by the lease of two more important roads, owned by the Ridge Avenue Company and the Thirteenth & Fifteenth Sts. Company.

The substitution of electric traction for horse power furnished an occasion for the consolidation of the independent lines which the Philadelphia Traction Company had not captured. In 1892 the Frankford & Southwark Company leased the lines of the Citizens Company. In 1893 it effected a consolidation with the Lombard & South Sts. Company and leased the road of the Second & Third Sts. Company. Then in the same year the Frankford & Southwark system, thus created, was leased by a new corporation, the Electric Traction Company. The Electric Traction Company at once purchased a controlling interest in the Omnibus Company, General, which was chartered in 1889, and has the privilege of running omnibuses on any street in Philadelphia, although it has only operated a line on Broad Street. Thus there was formed a system next in importance to that of the Philadelphia Traction Company.

In 1893 the People's Traction Company was organized to operate the lines of the People's Passenger Railway Company,[1] which it proceeded to equip with electric motive power.

After the extensive consolidation movement of 1893 there was left unabsorbed only one original company, the Hestonville, Mantua & Fairmount Passenger Railway Company. All of the other companies had become part of one of three great systems, the Philadelphia Traction, the Electric Traction, and the People's Traction. The relative importance of these systems and the single independent company is represented in the following statement for the year ending June 30, 1895:

	Miles of Track.	Passengers Carried.	Total Receipts.
Philadelphia Traction Co. ...	203	111,475,982	$5,662,051
Electric Traction Co.	130	58,125,481	2,151,853
People's Traction Co.	73	44,927,760	1,678,087
H. M. & F. P. R. Co.	24	7,560,094	373,690

It was not difficult to foresee the next move. Three traction companies had consolidated the interests of the eighteen independent companies of twenty years before. The advantages of the consolidation that had been effected were evident to the managers, and the wastes of competitive operation of the three systems were apparent to the most casual observer. Three distinct trolley wires strung side by side over a bit of track used in common by all three traction companies furnished a hint of the waste which

---

[1] See p. 31.

was incident to separate plants for the generation of power. Three distinct sets of administrative officers, too many cars on certain lines, and various other extravagancies of competition obtruded themselves upon the managers and the public alike. The result was inevitable. It came quickly.

During the spring of 1895 the next and final step in consolidation was foreshadowed by the passage of three important acts[1] by the General Assembly. The first of these authorized traction companies to enter into contract with each other for the sale, lease or operation of their respective property and franchises. The second authorized passenger railway companies to sell or lease all or any part of their property and franchises to traction companies and make contracts with traction companies for the operation of their lines. This act was designed to remove all doubt which had arisen regarding the legality of the leases and sales of franchise privileges of passenger railway companies to traction companies, which had already taken place in numerous instances. The third act authorized traction or railway companies owning, leasing, controlling or operating different lines to operate the lines as a general system and to lay out new routes over the streets occupied.

The expected happened very promptly. On July 22, 1895, a preliminary conference was held at which a plan of consolidation of the Philadelphia companies was discussed, and on September 6 the Union Traction Company was chartered with an authorized capital of $30,000,000. The stock of the Electric Traction Company and the People's Traction Company was bought by the new corporation, and the system of the Philadelphia Traction was leased.[2] July 1, 1896, the Electric Traction and the People's Traction were also leased by the Union Traction in order that the Union Company might acquire the direct management of

---

[1] Acts of May 15, 1895.
[2] For terms of purchase and lease see pp. 45 and 46.

all the lines. Thus the Union Traction Company came into control of the entire street railway system of Philadelphia with the exception of one line with twenty-four miles of track, owned and operated by a company incorporated in 1859, the Hestonville, Mantua & Fairmount Passenger Railway Co.

Thus was the doctrine of natural monopoly vindicated in Philadelphia.

CHAPTER IV.

FINANCIAL ASPECTS.

A thoroughly satisfactory treatment of the financial results of the Philadelphia street railway system is impossible at the present time, because many of the facts essential for a complete presentation of the subject cannot be obtained. The managers of the railways publish very meagre financial statements, and the public has never effectively demanded full reports. Pennsylvania has no Board of Railroad Commissioners to supervise the railways and publish their accounts. The companies are obliged to make annually to the Auditor-General of the State sworn reports, on the basis of which the State taxation on capital stock and gross receipts is levied, but these statements are withheld from the public on the ground that they are confidential. The Secretary of Internal Affairs publishes a report on railroads which purports to give the facts regarding stock, debt, cost of equipment, gross receipts, operating expenses, dividend payments and other matters of importance, but the statements are made in the form of incomplete and confused summaries that are of little value. The investigator who attempts to work from the statements of the Secretary of Internal Affairs speedily arrives at the conclusion of the street railway expert who condemns the railway reports of Pennsylvania as "in the highest degree chaotic, inconsistent and misleading."

The history of the publication of financial statements of street railways in Pennsylvania is interesting and significant. At the beginning of the development of the system, detailed sworn statements of all the facts of interest in connection with the equipment and operation of the railways were published annually by the Auditor-General. The earlier reports show some important omissions on the part of a few of the railway companies, which are frankly indicated, but on the whole the facts are given with satisfactory fullness of detail.

In 1874 the published statements of the railways were transferred from the reports of the Auditor-General to those of the Secretary of Internal Affairs, but until 1883 the character of the reports did not suffer from the transfer. Then in 1883, the Secretary, Mr. J. Simpson Africa, says in the introduction to his report that the public will be surprised to find the volume on railroads and street railways issued by his department less complete and less satisfactory than usual. In explanation he calls attention to the law of June 4, 1883, which required that the number of copies of the report of the department be limited to 2500, and that the maximum number of pages be 500. The reason for the passage of this act, which made it impossible to adequately present facts of interest and importance to the public, does not appear in the statute.

Immediately after this the published reports of the Philadelphia companies became valueless. Not only was the form of the report meagre, but in many cases there was no pretense of reporting the few facts required by the form. A star in a blank space in the summaries simply referred the investigator to a foot-note—" Not reported."

It is not without significance that this change in the form of the report was coincident with the organization of the Philadelphia Traction Company, which was chartered for the purpose of acquiring by purchase and lease the lines of several of the original passenger railway companies. A very slight knowledge of the brilliant financial operations of that period makes it clear that the change in the method of reporting which the State officials made at that time must have been most convenient and agreeable to the organizers of the new system. It would have greatly embarrassed some of the cleverest operations of street railway financiering in Philadelphia if the public had been in possession of all the facts.

In recent years the official reports have improved somewhat, but they are still very unsatisfactory.¹ However, within the past few years the extraordinary interest of investors and public alike in street railway properties, due largely to the revolution in service resulting from the application of electricity to traction, with its consequent enormous expansion of street railway investments, has furnished a motive for careful investigation of the real return to such enterprises.² In Philadelphia the task of investigation has been exceedingly difficult, owing to the complicated stock, bond and lease operations extending over many years, the terms of which have been carefully concealed from the public. But enough is now known to make possible somewhat close approximations to the financial results of the Philadelphia railways.

From the very beginning Philadelphia street railway stock has been most remunerative property. In 1859 there was published a "Treatise on Street or Horse-power Railways,"³ in the preface of which the author says: "The following, I hope, will be the means of inciting investigation to a system which, although now in its infancy, is rapidly providing a secure and profitable investment for a large amount of

---

[1] The experience of the Pennsylvania public in failing to obtain information regarding the financial condition of its street railways is not unique. Very few of the States have published satisfactory reports of the railway systems of their cities. The failure of the public to demand vitally important information which they have the undoubted right to exact is a striking illustration of that characteristic American apathy which is largely responsible for corporate aggression on public rights. However, there has been improvement in this respect recently, and several States are beginning to furnish reasonably complete reports. The Massachusetts reports are the best, the Railroad Commissioners of that State prescribing the form of accounting for the railways, thus preventing the companies from concealing their real condition by bookkeeping expedients. The New York reports are also excellent, the form of accounting being carefully controlled.

[2] A recent estimate places the total capitalization of street railways in the United States at $1,375,300,000; of this amount, $784,800,000 is capital stock and $590,500,000 indebtedness.

[3] Easton—A Practical Treatise on Street or Horse-Power Railways. Phila., 1859.

capital." He proceeds to show that the net profit for one year on $5,044,520 invested in four railways in New York City and four in Boston was $638,911, or 12.4 per cent., and then says: " No returns have yet been made of the operations of the many railways laid down in Philadelphia, but from actual observation it is calculated that the aggregate of their incomes will, in proportion to the amount invested, far exceed that of Boston and New York." He cites the fact that the stockholders of the Philadelphia and Darby Passenger Railway Company had already declined to entertain a proposal to lease their road for five years for a net return of 8 per cent. on their investment; and says that the Citizens Passenger Railway Company, " which was considered the most desperate of all undertakings," declared a dividend of 8.5 per cent. in five months.

Among the large numbers of companies chartered at the outset when " passenger railway insanity " held sway among the investors, there were a few that were not profitable, but most of the railways made ample return to the stockholders from the moment that they were put into operation, and several began to make very large profits at once. The following table shows the paid-in capital and dividend payment for the five most profitable companies and for all companies, for the year ending November 30, 1864.

	Paid-in Capital Stock.	Dividend.	Per cent. of Dividend on Paid-in Capital Stock.
Philadelphia City	$ 100,000	45,000	45.0
Second & Third Sts.	203,757	56,990	27.9
Citizens	192,750	41,825	21.7
Green & Coates	150,000	31,084	20.7
Girard College	160,000	20,000	12.5
All companies	3,127,694	310,467	9.9

Thus soon after the system was fairly in operation, four companies paid over 20 per cent. dividends and the average return on the investment in all companies was about 10 per cent. As the city developed and the traffic grew, the dividend return increased rapidly.

The financial development of the railways is exhibited by the following table, which presents the most important facts regarding the entire Philadelphia system for the years indicated. The figures are taken from the reports of the Auditor-General and the Secretary of Internal Affairs for the earlier years, and from a variety of available sources, official and private, for the later years. The table is not entirely accurate, since the information on which it is based is not complete, but it indicates in a general way the development of the system on its financial side.

Year.	Miles of Track.	Passengers.	Paid-in Capital Stock.	Total Debt.	Cost of Construction and Equipment.	Cash Dividend	Percentage of Dividend on paid-in Capital Stock.
1864	129	44,624,710	$3,127,694	$1,407,195	$4,286,680	$310,467	9.9%
1869	177	56,804,392	4,326,239	1,311,634	5,911,074	456,114	10.5%
1874	230	78,489,131	5,326,998	2,167,393	7,899,737	960,444	18.0%
1880	298	99,045,515	6,468,459	3,049,935	9,758,455	1,181,100	18.2%
1885	319	117,171,681	10,388,096	4,062,058	*	1,823,885	17.5%
1890	345	164,542,586	12,832,036	6,491,636	*	2,243,401	17.5%
1895	436	224,238,116	40,654,838[1]	7,322,635	25,730,981	3,249,440	8.0%

* Official figures so incomplete that no estimate is possible.

Until 1884 the Philadelphia railway properties had been directly controlled by a large number of comparatively small stockholders, the stock being widely scattered in small blocks throughout the community. But in 1884 a new era in the financial history of Philadelphia railways was inaugurated by the Philadelphia Traction Company, which entered the field as an operating company for existing railways. It at once assumed the operation under lease of two important systems, paying all fixed charges and guaranteeing large dividends. Later, when the change in motive power from horses to electricity was accomplished, the Philadelphia

---

[1] Does not include Union Traction stock. The large increase from 1890 is explained by the heavy issues of the traction companies and by the reconstruction for electric motive power.

Traction Company and two new traction companies chartered in 1893 extended the policy of acquiring the operation of lines by leasing the original companies under guaranteed dividend, until by 1895 all but one of the railway companies had been attached to one of the three large traction systems.

The very large profit on actual investment in Philadelphia railways is registered in the price which these operating companies pay for the privilege of exercising the franchises of the original companies. The following table shows the net return which the present stockholders of the original railway companies are receiving on paid-in capital stock under guarantee of the operating traction companies.

The lease terms of the principal lines of the Philadelphia Traction system provide for net return on paid-in capital stock as follows:

Name of Company.	Annual Dividend on paid-in Capital Stock.
Continental	20.7%
Philadelphia City	31.5
Philadelphia & Gray's Ferry	16.0
Ridge Avenue	42.8
Thirteenth & Fifteenth Sts.	65.6[1]
Union	31.6
West Philadelphia	20.0

The dividend charges of the Electric Traction Company are as follows:

Frankford & Southwark	27%[2]
Citizens	67[3]
Second & Third Sts.	25[4]

The People's Traction Company has pledged the following dividends on paid-in capital stock:

Germantown	24%
Green & Coates Sts.	40

---

[1] To be increased to 71.6% after 1900.
[2] To be increased to 36% by 1903.
[3] To be increased to 72% after 1899.
[4] To be increased to 30% by 1903.

Financial Aspects.

The January, 1897, quotations of stock of the companies just considered and of the two traction companies, the stock of which is on the market, are as follows:

Name of Company.	Par Value.	Amount paid in per Share.	Market Price.
Continental	50	29	131
Philadelphia City	50	23.75	172
Philadelphia & Gray's Ferry.	50	25	82½
Ridge Avenue	50	28	244
Thirteenth & Fifteenth Sts.	50	16.75	227½
Union Passenger Railway	50	30	210
West Philadelphia	50	50	219
Frankford & Southwark	50	50	334
Citizens	50	19.40 (average)[1]	272
Second & Third Sts.	50	40	237
Germantown	50	21.66 (average)[2]	125
Green & Coates Sts.	50	15	132¼
Philadelphia Traction	50	50	69⅝
Union Traction	50	10	9½

The present market value of the stocks of all the street railway companies of Philadelphia exceeds $120,000,000; the amount of paid capital stock, including that of the traction companies, being in the vicinity of $50,000,000; while the total cost of the construction and equipment of the roads which the stocks represent is about $36,000,000.

An analysis of the obligations assumed by the Union Traction Company through its purchase of the stock of the People's Traction Company throws some light upon the process of inflation of values in street railway stocks. Fifteen years ago the People's Passenger Railway Company built up an extensive system of railways by the lease of the Germantown Company at 26 per cent. annual rental on paid-in capital, and a lease of the Green & Coates Sts. Company at an annual rental of 40 per cent. on paid-in capital. Burdened by these enormous lease charges, the stock of the People's Passenger Railway Company, with $11.30 per share paid in, was sold in 1893 to the People's Traction Company at $75 per share. Now the People's Traction Com-

---

[1] 8500 shares of $20 paid, and 1500 shares of $16 paid.
[2] 10,000 shares of $35 paid, and 20,000 shares of $15 paid.

pany has sold its stock in turn to the Union Traction Company for $76 per share, $30 having been paid per share. In other words, the Union Traction Company has paid $76 per share for stock which represents an actual investment of $30, in order to obtain from the People's Traction Company the privilege of operating the People's Passenger Railway Company under the condition of 4 per cent. interest on $75 for every $11.30 which was actually invested in the railway, and in addition paying dividends of 40 per cent. and 26 per cent. respectively on the investment in two leased roads. By these transactions the Union Traction has undertaken to pay interest on a capitalization of about $21,000,000 for the right to operate a railway system which has cost for construction and equipment $6,830,425.

The foregoing consideration, in connection with the facts regarding guaranteed dividends and market price of stocks already quoted, indicate how excessive are the profits derived by the stockholders of the original companies and how heavy is the burden of fixed charges carried by the present operating companies. The railway companies holding perpetual franchises, which are constantly becoming more valuable through the growth of the city, were in a position to exact from the traction companies a large payment for franchise rights. In cities more wise or more fortunate than Philadelphia, where franchises are not granted in perpetuity, but are limited to twenty or thirty-year periods, such excessive profits as those now paid by the traction companies on the stock of the original companies flow into the city treasury or are distributed in the form of lower fares.

The present value of the franchise privileges given by the city to its railways, as estimated by the able financiers who effected the recent consolidation, is of much interest to the public and is easily ascertained. The Union Traction Company reports an annual expenditure of about $5,463,000 as fixed charges. These fixed charges are made up of two elements. The first is the payment for the use of existing railways and equipment, and the second is the amount exacted by the stockholders of the constituent companies as payment for the franchise privileges bestowed upon them by the city. The amount of the first element in the fixed charges is readily calculated. The companies report the cost of construction and equipment of the railway system as $34,156,000, which is apparently an outside estimate. The interest at 5 per cent. on this cost is $1,707,800, which may be taken as a fair return on the capital actually invested in the roads. The second element in the fixed charges must then amount to $3,755,000, and this sum thus represents the annual payment guaranteed by the Union Traction Company for the simple right to use the locations granted to the original companies by the city of Philadelphia. This payment is an interest charge of 5 per cent. on $75,100,000, and this amount is consequently the present approximate value of the gift to the city to its railway companies. In return for these exclusive privileges, which are valued by the company at $75,000,000, the city and the State receive in taxation $1,163,000 annually.

The existing combination of street railway lines, the Union Traction Company, dates from the fall of 1895. At the time of consolidation there were in existence three great traction companies, which were controlling and operating all the original railway companies save one. These were the Philadelphia Traction Company, first organized in 1883 and rechartered in 1888; the People's Traction Company, incorporated in March, 1893; and the Electric Traction Company, incorporated in May, 1893.

The Union Traction Company was organized with a capital of $30,000,000 in $50 shares. The plan of organization provided for the purchase of the stock of the Electric Traction Company at $85 per share for the full-paid $50 shares and $70 per share for the shares on which $30 had been paid; and also for the purchase of the People's Traction Company stock, $30 paid, at $76 per share. These shares were paid for with 4 per cent. collateral trust gold certificates, not redeemable before 1945. In addition, the Union Company leased all rights, property and franchises of the Philadelphia Traction Company for 999 years at a net rental of 8 per cent. on capital stock. Finally, on July 1, 1896, the Union Traction Company leased the lines of the People's and Electric Companies, whose stock it held in trust, in order to assume directly the operation of the roads, the consideration being the amount of the interest on the Electric and People's Trust Certificates.

By the terms of the agreement the shareholders of the three constituent traction companies had the right to purchase the stock of the Union Traction Company in proportion to their several holdings. The speculative value of this right appears from the fact that immediately after the Union Traction Company completed its purchase and lease the stock was quoted at $14 per share, $5 being paid-in value.[1]

The present earning capacity of the railways now consolidated by the Union Traction Company is shown by the following table, which gives the figures for the year ending June 30, 1896. The figures quoted cover companies which operate nearly 95 per cent. of the railway mileage of Philadelphia.

Companies.	Gross Earnings.	Operating Expenses.	Net Earnings.	Cost of Road and Equipment.
Electric Traction,	$2,496,164	$1,270,208	$1,225,956	$7,787,713
People's Traction,	2,035,082	1,084,892	950,190	6,830,425
Phila. Traction,	5,678,780	3,007,926	2,670,854	19,538,378
	$10,210,026	$5,363,026	$4,847,000	$34,156,516

A glance at these figures shows that the present earning power of the Philadelphia companies is large. With the longest lines of any surface system in the country, the gross receipts per mile of track are above $24,000. This return on the basis of track mileage is exceeded by only four of

---

[1] The stock has since declined to 9⅞ on paid-in value of $10.

the seventeen surface systems of this country which operate 100 miles or more of track.[1]

But even with this large earning capacity, the present organization of the railways is maintained with difficulty, because of the heavy over-capitalization of the system. The capitalization of the Union Traction Company and constituent companies is estimated as follows:[2]

Constituent Companies:
    Capital stock $57,891,200
    Funded debt 11,675,600
Union Traction Co.:
    Capital stock 30,000,000
    Collateral Trust 4s. 29,735,000
                               —————$129,301,800
    Less stock in trust 21,000,000

        Total net capitalization $108,301,800

Thus the 447 miles of track of the Union Traction Company are capitalized at $242,280 per mile.[3] The cost of con-

[1] Companies.	Miles Track.	Total Receipts.	Per Mile Track.
Metropolitan Co., N. Y.	189	$9,131,000	$48,200
West End Co., Boston.........	263	7,746,171	29,400
North Chicago Co., Chicago...	100	2,780,487	27,805
Chicago City Co., Chicago.....	162	4,476,824	27,500
Union Traction Co., Phila......	420	10,210,026	24,300

The figures for the Metropolitan and Union companies are for the year ending June 30, 1896; for the two Chicago companies for the year ending December 31, 1895; and for the Boston company for the year ending June 30, 1895. These comparative figures are taken from an article by Mr. Edward E. Higgins, in the Street Railway Journal of October, 1896.

[2] This is the estimate of L. H. Taylor & Co., bankers, in a circular issued August 10, 1895, urging the ratification of the proposed consolidation. The figures have been endorsed by representatives of the company as substantially correct.

[3] Excessive as is this capitalization per mile of track, it is exceeded by that of three surface railways in the United States, the figures being as follows:

Companies.	Miles of Track.	Total Capitalization.	Capitalization per Mile.
Third Ave. Co., N. Y.	28	$14,000,000	$493,000
Capital Traction Co., Wash., D. C..	36	12,000,000	333,300
Metropolitan Co., N. Y.	189	54,884,000	280,900
Union Co., Phila.	447	108,301,800	242,200

struction and equipment, including paving of the streets occupied by the tracks, as reported by the companies, is $76,400 per mile of track.[1] The lines are thus capitalized at more than three times their reported cost of construction and equipment.

It is clear that a system thus over-capitalized and burdened with the lease charges quoted must be managed with consummate skill in order to make a profit for the operating company. The gross receipts of the system for the year ending June 30, 1896, were $10,210,026. The fixed charges representing rental of roads and interest on indebtedness were $5,463,051, while taxes and licenses are estimated at $800,000 per annum. Thus according to the statement of the Company in its annual report, the payment of fixed charges and taxes would leave only about 40 per cent. of the gross receipts for operating expenses, while the report of the Company for nine months ending June 30, 1896, shows that the operating expenses were 52¾, 53⅓, and 56¼ per cent. of the total receipts respectively for the three traction systems.

In the absence of detailed information as to the resources of the Company and the exact basis upon which the figures presented are calculated, it is impossible to predict the outcome, but it is beyond question that the managers of the Union Traction Company are facing a very serious financial

---

The important systems in United States and Canada having the smallest capitalization per mile of track are as follows:

Companies.	Miles of Track.	Total Capitalization.	Capitalization per Mile.
Montreal Ry. Co.	75	$ 5,000,000	$66,500
Louisville Ry. Co.	150	12,000,000	80,000
Buffalo Ry. Co.	142	12,507,000	84,700
Lindell Ry. Co., St. Louis	60	5,400,000	89,800
West End Co., Boston	263	23,705,000	90,000

[1] For purposes of comparison with cost of construction and equipment of other systems the special paving charge estimated at $9,000,000 should be deducted. This makes the cost of the roads and equipment about $56,300 per mile. The cost of construction and equipment of Massachusetts street railways, as reported in 1895, varied from $11,737 to $97,904 per mile, averaging $48,729 per mile of main track.

problem. President Welsh reported that the first nine months of operation of the present system ending June 30, 1896, showed a loss of $1,045,246, but that accrued dividends on stock owned by the Company made the net deficit only $49,293. It is not known on what basis the accrued dividends were calculated. The president of the Company in his first annual report gives the stockholders no definite assurance for the future, simply saying: "It is unnecessary to remind stockholders that the conditions have not been favorable for business during the period under review, owing to the great depression which has existed in most branches of trade and other well-known causes."

The present financial organization of the Union Traction Company is apparently justified only by faith in large expansion of traffic in the near future. The fixed charges representing payment to the original companies for franchise privileges increase slightly during the next few years, but after 1903 there will be no increase in this item of expense. Meantime the gross receipts will become progressively larger as the city grows, and thus a balance may be expected to appear on the right side of the ledger. The managers of the Company have discounted this future increase of net revenue in the present financial arrangement, and are doubtless struggling with the present deficit sustained by hope of future profit if the organization can meantime be maintained.

The financial aspect of street railway service which most interests the general public is the rate of fare.[1] In the

---

[1] The railway companies of Philadelphia began in 1858 with a five cent fare. The usual omnibus rate had been six cents, and the railways promised a reduction, urging this as one reason for establishing the new system of transportation. At first, exchange tickets were sold for six cents, but in 1860 the exchange rate was made seven cents by the Board of Railway Presidents.

Although there were many attempts to change the rate, the single fare remained at five cents until 1864, when it was increased to six cents. The reason given for the increase was the "high price of horse feed."

Shortly after this the single fare was increased to seven cents, attempt to increase the gross earnings of the system, the Union Traction Company adopted a new policy with reference to fares as soon as it assumed control. Philadelphia is a city of right angles, and most of the lines had run directly east and west or north and south. Thus the proportion of riders who were obliged to change from one line to another to reach their destination was very large. Each of the three traction systems before the consolidation gave transfer privileges very freely for a single five cent fare, the newer companies, the People's Traction and the Electric Traction, being especially liberal in this regard. There were about 350 transfer points in the city, and it is estimated that about 40 per cent. of the patrons of the cars called for passes. One of the first moves of the Union Traction Company was the abolition of free transfers and the establishment of a universal eight-cent exchange rate.

The change in the customary rate of fare for a large proportion of the patrons naturally met with vigorous protest on the part of the public and gave rise to a movement to secure a general free transfer system or to force a reduction of the single fare to four, or even three, cents if possible. The popular feeling is reflected by the grand jury for November, 1895, which presented the consolidation of the companies and the consequent abolition of free transfers as a public evil, and urged that the legality of the combination be tested. No concessions in the way of lower fare or free transfers were made by the Company, however, and it seems probable from the foregoing review of financial conditions

---

16 tickets being offered for one dollar, and exchange tickets for nine cents each. These rates were maintained for about twelve years, and then, in January, 1877, the fare was reduced to six cents, the price of exchange tickets remaining nine cents.

Four years later, in 1881, the general demand for cheaper transportation induced Councils to attach to a grant of extension privileges, requested by the Lombard and South Sts. Co., the condition of a five cent fare. As other companies applied for privileges Councils took similar action in many cases, and later the General Assembly made the five cent rate a condition of using cable traction. Thus by means of the pressure brought to bear by the public a uniform five cent rate was attained in 1887.

that no important concessions can be made in the immediate future without destroying the basis of the present organization.[1]

It is not without significance in this connection that the stock of the railway companies and the trust certificates which were issued in payment for the stock of the People's and Electric Companies purchased by the Union Company are quite widely distributed throughout the community in small blocks. Recent transactions indicate clearly that it is the policy of the managers of the Union Company to get its securities into the hands of a large number of small holders, the plain inference being that the officials feel that a wide distribution of securities will fortify the Company against possible attack by the public. The man who holds the stocks or bonds of the companies is naturally a defender of the present organization, and in the event of a contest a large body of security holders would be a source of great strength to the Company. In the recent struggle over the question of fares the "thousands of frugal and comparatively poor people who have their savings invested in the shares of these corporations" were made to play an important role in the defense of the Company. A prominent director said in a newspaper interview, "Our critics have engaged the Academy of Music and wish to call an assemblage of people opposed to street railways as now managed. It would take eight Academies of Music to hold the stockholders of the Union Traction Company, whose interests to-day are being assailed by wanton attacks upon the most commendable business enterprise that I know of in this country. . . . There are about twenty-five thousand of them."[2] The value to the Company of the conservative

---

[1] When the free transfer system was abolished the Company promised to rearrange its routes and establish several L lines, thus reducing the necessary number of transfers. This promise has been fulfilled and it is now possible to reach the business center of the city from every section of Philadelphia for a single fare. The lines have also been so arranged that Fairmount Park can be reached from most sections for five cents.

[2] Mr. Thomas Dolan in *Philadelphia Times*, Nov. 29, 1895.

force of the large body of citizens financially interested in the maintenance of the present organization will be readily appreciated.

Meantime, realizing the very large return which the present rate of fare yields on the legitimate investment in the railways, and noting the tendency towards decrease of fare in other cities, the public feels that its present cost of transportation service is excessive, and many are anxious to test the reserved right of purchase or the power of Councils to force a reduction of fare. Manifestly only the wisest management can meet successfully the varied and exacting demands of public and stockholders.

CHAPTER V.

THE PRICE OF FRANCHISE PRIVILEGES.

Having reviewed the facts showing the return which the street railways have made to investors, we are prepared to consider the price which they have paid to the city for their franchise privileges.

In order to secure for the city some remuneration for the privilege of constructing and operating street railways in Philadelphia, three obligations were imposed upon the companies by charter and ordinance. These obligations are (1) to "pave, repave and repair" the streets which they occupy; (2) to pay to the city a tax on annual dividends in excess of 6 per cent.,[1] and (3) to pay a license fee for each car "intended to be run."

Unfortunately, from 1857 to 1874, each company was chartered by special act of the General Assembly, and the thirty-nine charters granted during this period differ widely in the form of obligation imposed. In 1873 the State Constitution was revised and a clause inserted forbidding special or local legislation. A general incorporation act was accordingly passed, April 29, 1874, and an act providing for the incorporation of passenger railway companies was placed on the statute books, May 14, 1889. However, most of the available territory had been granted during the era of special legislation, so all the important companies of the present day are operating under special charters.

The different terms of the charters prior to 1874 made it difficult for the city to define and enforce the financial obligations of the companies to the city, and were fruitful sources of vexatious legislation. The complications thus

---

[1] Imposed on fifteen of the eighteen companies in independent existence in 1874. None of the companies chartered since 1874 are liable to this dividend tax.

arising make it necessary to examine each one of the obligations separately and in some detail.

I. *The Paving Obligation.*—The most important return which the companies have made to the city for their privileges has been the paving and maintenance of all streets occupied by their tracks. Every company but one[1] assumed this obligation to pave and repave or to repair the streets, or both.

The charter provisions on this subject vary quite widely. Some expressly provide that "said company shall pave and keep in good repair such portion of the street as may be occupied by said railway." Another form runs, "Provided it shall keep the streets, through which said railway passes, so far as said railway shall run along said street, in perpetual good repair at the proper expense of said company." Another common form is less definite, merely declaring, "Said Councils may by ordinances establish such regulations in regard to said railway as may be required for paving, repaving, grading, culverting of and laying gas and water pipes in and along such streets." Some of the charters made no reference to the care of the streets.

Ordinance provisions, however, made the paving obligation definite and in connection with charter provisions imposed upon all but five of the companies the duty of paving, repaving and repairing streets which they occupy.[2] In most cases, the consent of Councils was required by charter before the lines could be built, and the companies that asked consent of the local legislature were obliged to file a written agreement to accept and observe the ordinance of 1857, which contained the paving requirement, and all other ordinances to be made by Councils for their control.

---

[1] Phila. and Darby Co.

[2] In October, 1896, the Supreme Court decided that under their charter provisions the obligation of the Hestonville, Mantua and Fairmount Co., the Empire Co., the Continental Co., and the Seventeenth and Nineteenth Sts. Co. is simply to repair and not to repave streets.

In other cases the charters required that the companies should be subject to all ordinances providing for their regulation, thus bringing them under the paving provision.

The section of the ordinance of 1857 which deals with the subject of paving is as follows: "All railroad companies, as aforesaid, shall be at the entire cost and expense of maintaining, paving, repairing and repaving that may be necessary upon any road, street, avenue or alley occupied by them." This provision was amended in 1859 in such a way as to relieve the companies from the duty of paving streets which were not paved at the time the tracks were laid.

The expression of the obligation is thus perfectly definite, but in spite of this fact the city has had great difficulty in forcing the companies to fulfill their contracts.

As late as 1887, thirty years after the passage of the ordinance and its acceptance by the earlier companies, we learn from a message of Mayor Fitler to Councils that the question of the responsibility of the city passenger railway companies to repave the streets with such pavement as modern necessities demand is still pending in the courts; that meantime the citizens are suffering, and consequently he proposes to lay before Councils a compromise plan for repaving under which the city and the companies shall share the burden. And it was four years later, in 1891, that the question of the enforcement of the contract obligations of the companies as to paving was definitely decided in favor of the city.

Until 1892, when, under conditions to be described later, improved pavement was laid on an extensive scale, Philadelphia was generally known as the worst paved city in America. The pavements were of roughest cobble stone, badly laid and sadly neglected. A partial explanation of this state of affairs is found in the history of the manner in which the railway companies discharged their paving obligations.

One of the first official references to the paving contract

is that of Mayor Henry in a message to Councils in January, 1859. He said, "There should be no unnecessary delay in the adoption of an ordinance which shall clearly define the obligations of the several companies to keep in constant repair the entire width of the streets occupied by them." The companies were already attempting to evade the terms of their contract by a claim that the proper interpretation of the charter and ordinance provisions required them to pave and maintain only that portion of the street actually occupied and used by them, viz., the space between the tracks.

In response to the Mayor's recommendation, Councils enacted the passenger railway ordinance of 1859, amending the original ordinance of 1857, and, among other changes, providing that the companies must repave or repair any street occupied by them on notice from the Chief Commissioner of Highways. In the event of failure on the part of the companies to comply with the request, the Chief Commissioner is authorized to do the work himself and place a bill for the amount expended in the hands of the City Solicitor for collection. After the passage of this ordinance we find in the finance reports of the city under the expenditure of the Department of Highways an item, "For repairing and repaving streets in which passenger railways are laid." The amounts annually placed opposite this item vary from a few dollars to a maximum of $247,481.75 in 1890. Up to 1889 the largest annual expenditure for this purpose was $9,060.07 in 1873, and the total amount was not large. But from 1889 to 1894 inclusive, the amount expended by the city on streets, which should have been cared for by the passenger railway companies, was $461,086. As we shall see later,[1] the city has recently recovered the larger part of the amount expended on streets occupied by the railways.

In 1865 we have in a message of the Mayor a revelation as to the spirit in which the companies were performing

---

[1] See p. 61.

their paving obligations. In April, 1865, Mayor Henry says: "The occupancy of many of the principal streets by passenger railway companies has devolved by ordinance the repair of their entire roadway upon the respective companies. The result of such an arrangement, as could have been anticipated, has been the prevalent neglect of the street pavement except within or immediately adjacent to the rails." It does not apparently occur to the Mayor that it is possible to enforce the contract obligations of the companies, for he proposes that the city resume control of all paving and charge the companies a "due proportion of expense."

The references to the bad condition of the streets are numerous in the messages of the various mayors. Meantime we note frequent ordinances instructing the companies to repave certain specified streets. There are also several directing the Chief Commissioner of Highways to do work which the companies have refused to do and to put in the hands of the Solicitor for collection, claims against the companies for the amounts expended.

Occasionally Councils reflect a popular agitation for better paved streets, and attempt radical reform. Thus, for instance, we find on March 7, 1874, an ordinance instructing the Chief Commissioner of Highways to notify all city passenger railway companies to repair highways which they occupy and to report the result in May. Councils did not rest content with this, for on March 23, 1874, the City Solicitor is directed to notify the presidents and directors of all companies that within ten days of the receipt of notice they must repair streets along their respective routes, and the Solicitor is further directed to prosecute officers who refuse to act. A somewhat similar ordinance was passed in 1876, Councils evidently desiring to have Philadelphia make a good impression on the numerous visitors of the Centennial Exposition. The last ordinance was evidently effective, for the report of the Department of Highways for 1876 speaks with approval of the large amount of work done by the companies during that year.

This activity of the companies was coincident with an important legal definition of their obligations. Acting under the ordinance referred to above, the Chief Commissioner of Highways had poled off a portion of a street and proceeded to repair it, meantime stopping the cars. The company asked for an injunction against the action of the Commissioner of Highways. In delivering the opinion of the Court dismissing the application for an injunction, President Judge Thayer laid down some most important principles.[1] In view of the later attitude of the companies, this judicial assertion of the right of the city is worthy of extended quotation even in a brief treatment of the subject. After a statement of charter and ordinance provisions, Judge Thayer said: "This review of the legislation of the State and of the City, in its bearing upon the relative rights and obligations of this railway Company and the City, results in several clear and indubitable conclusions:

First. That this Company are bound to keep in repair the entire roadway of the streets which they occupy—not only the part between the rails, but the whole roadway, from curb to curb. . . . Whatever streets they traverse they are bound to pave throughout their whole route, and that not partially, but wholly and thoroughly. . . . It is a part of the price which the Legislature exacted for the privileges granted. And the privileges, I may add, were cheaply purchased at the price imposed. . . .

Second. Another conclusion deducible from the legislation in reference to this Company is, that they are not only bound by the ordinance of 1857, but also by all other ordinances passed by the city. They are not only bound by the express words of their charter to obey the ordinance of 1857, but it results from their charter also, and from their own solemn agreement, made with the city in pursuance of it, that they are equally bound by all other ordinances passed, or to be passed, so always, of course, that they be

---

[1] Phila. and Gray's Ferry Pass. Ry. Co. vs. Phila., 11 Phila. Reports, 358.

reasonable and lawful in their nature. The privileges of this Company were, by the very fiat of its creation, to depend upon the will of the city. It could slay or it could make alive. It was armed with power to strangle it at its birth, or to nurse it into useful strength and vigor. This power was given to the city for a salutary purpose; for a public and beneficial purpose. That purpose was to subordinate the corporate existence of the Company to the laws of the community in which it was to live—to protect the municipal rights and liberties of the City of Philadelphia. The stockholders of the Company unanimously voted that they were willing to be so bound. They entered into a solemn contract with the city, under their corporate seal, and the hands of their chief officers, binding themselves to be subject to all ordinances of the city, passed or to be passed. They now attempt to repudiate that obligation, and assert that the city had no right to impose that condition, and that they are not bound by it. I cannot acquiesce in so bold an assumption. That the city had the right to impose this condition, as the consideration of its assent to the charter, and that the Company, having obtained that consent by means of their contract with the city to be bound by its ordinances, cannot now repudiate that contract or escape from it, seems to me to be a conclusion founded not only upon principles of sound reason and common honesty, but grounded also upon the firmest rules of law."

In 1883 we are informed by the report of J. D. Estabrook, Chief Commissioner of Highways, that the streets of the city were in unusually bad condition. Notices were sent to the companies that repairs must be undertaken, and in the language of the report, "The railway companies generally did a large amount of work, and soon put their streets in fair condition."[1]

---

[1] The amount of roadway thus put in fair condition appears from the following figures from the report of the Commissioner:
Total length of all streets in Philadelphia .... 1060.51 miles.
Total length of all paved streets .... 573.54 "
Total length paved streets occupied by railways 203.74 "

The response of the companies to the requirements of the Chief Commissioner to "mend their ways" in a double sense again coincides with a legal decision affirming their responsibility. The Navy Yard, Broad Street & Fairmount Passenger Railway Company had a provision in its charter requiring the company to keep in repair "that portion of the street which they use and occupy." This Company had consolidated with the Thirteenth & Fifteenth Sts. Passenger Railway Company, and suit in equity was now brought for injunction to prevent the Commissioner from stopping the running of the cars while the street, neglected by the Company, was being repaired by the city, on the ground that the correct interpretation of the charter required the Company to pave and keep in repair only the space between the tracks. The judgment of the case already cited was affirmed, the court holding that the words "that portion of the streets which they use and occupy" signified the length of street which they used.[1]

But the unwonted zeal of the companies is hardly to be attributed solely to the decision of the Court of Common Pleas. This was the period of the activity of the famous Committee of One Hundred, a body of citizens organized to deliver Philadelphia from the clutches of the Gas Ring, a worthy rival of Tammany in the arts of municipal corruption. In May, 1882, the Committee engaged an inspector of highways, and in the fall the Sub-Committee on Municipal Abuses made a report charging that gross irregularities existed in the management of the Department of Highways. The resulting investigation proved that great abuses indeed existed, and brought about partial reformation. It was in consequence of this agitation that the railway companies found it expedient to put their streets in "fair condition."

Soon the paving question assumed a new phase. Philadelphia was becoming ashamed of her antiquated cobble

---

[1] Thirteenth & Fifteenth Sts. Pass. Ry. Co. vs. Phila. & J. D. Estabrook, 16 Phila. Reports, 164.

stone pavements. In 1882 the city had only 281,055 square yards of Belgian block out of a total paved area of 7,921,055 square yards, the rest being cobble stones and rubble. The people began to feel keenly that the condition of the streets was far from creditable to a great municipality. Councils, responding to a popular demand, attempted to force the railway companies to repave the principal streets with improved paving material. May 6, 1886, the Commissioner of Highways was directed to order the Ridge Avenue Passenger Railway Company to repave with Belgian block a portion of one of the streets it occupied. The Company refused, and forthwith the city laid the pavement and brought suit to recover the amount expended. The Court of Common Pleas gave judgment for the city and defined the obligation of companies in unmistakable terms. The case was then appealed to the Supreme Court, and after a memorable legal battle the Supreme Court affirmed the judgment of the lower court.[1] The decision finally disposed of one of the claims of the companies thus: "It has never been seriously doubted, nor can it be, that the duty to repair or to repave, when either is adjudged necessary, extends to the entire roadway from curb to curb." And with reference to the obligation to lay improved pavement the decision is quite as explicit. "The company is bound to keep pace with the progress of the age in which it continues to exercise its corporate functions. The city authorities have just as much right to require it to repave at its own expense with a new, better and more expensive pavement, as they have to cause other streets to be repaved, in like manner, at the public expense." Under this decision the City Solicitor has collected about $475,000 of the amount expended by the city for paving streets occupied by the railways, the total amount claimed being $600,000.

Shortly after this decision was rendered, the companies sought from Councils authority to use the overhead electric

---

[1] Phila. vs. Ridge Av. Pass. Ry. Co., 143 Pa. State Reports, 444.

system of propulsion.[1] The first ordinances, granted early in 1892, and passed over the veto of the mayor, gave the important privilege asked without defining anew the obligations of the companies, but in later ordinances, conveying the same privilege and covering most of the lines, Councils, in response to irresistible popular demand, strengthened the hold of the municipality on the companies by attaching to the grants a definition of the obligations of the companies to the city. One of these ordinances is reprinted in the appendix, and the very explicit paving provision will be found there.

Under the new ordinances the railway companies in co-operation with the city began to effect a notable transformation in Philadelphia pavements. In 1892 the companies laid 10.25 miles of asphalt and Belgian block, and during 1893 they repaved with these materials 50.39 miles of streets at an estimated cost of over $2,000,000. Meantime the city laid 66.55 miles of modern pavement.

In 1894 a still larger amount of work was done. The railway companies laid 131.17 miles of street with improved pavement at a cost of about $5,000,000, as estimated by the Chief of the Bureau of Highways. At the close of 1896

---

[1] The request of the companies for the privilege of using the overhead trolley system of traction met with violent opposition from a large proportion of the citizens of Philadelphia. A Union Committee for Opposing the Trolley System, composed of prominent and influential citizens, conducted a vigorous campaign against the proposed change of motive power. The party of opposition undoubtedly contained a considerable element of unreflecting conservatives, but a much larger part were thoroughly intelligent remonstrants against the introduction of an overhead construction which was deemed dangerous to life and property, the intelligent opponents contending that it would be better to tolerate the old system for a short time until the underground trolley, the storage battery, compressed air, or some more desirable system of propulsion could be secured. Moreover, a considerable proportion of the opposition is explained by the prevalent distrust of the railway corporations and the consequent reluctance of the public to grant further favors to companies which had abused the privileges already conferred. This determined opposition forced the companies to make the important concessions noted above in order to secure the more profitable system of propulsion.

the Bureau estimates that 271 miles of street have been repaved by the companies since 1891 at a cost of about $9,000,000.

The change that has been wrought in Philadelphia by the co-operation of the companies and the city can be imagined when it is remembered that in 1891 the cobble stone pavement of medieval type was almost universal, while at the end of 1896 only 173 miles of cobble stone and rubble remained out of a total length of 812 miles of paved streets, exclusive of macadam.

Thus after nearly forty years of alternate neglect and partial performance of obligations, which were definitely assumed by most of the companies, and, it is safe to assert, clearly understood by both parties to the contract, the city of Philadelphia is at last in full enjoyment of the return which her representatives of a generation ago exacted as the greater part of the price of the valuable privileges they bestowed on street car companies.

The plain lesson derived from the foregoing sketch is that the imposition of an obligation upon street railway companies to pave and keep in repair the streets they traverse, is a most unwise and vexatious method of exacting a return for privileges granted. This fact is not apparent to Philadelphians at the present moment, for they are in the first flush of enjoyment of admirably paved streets. Almost the entire length of roadway traversed by the lines of the street car companies has been repaved within the past four years. The rapid transition from cobble stones to asphalt and Belgian block, which has transformed Philadelphia from one of the worst to one of the best paved cities in the United States, has induced a feeling of complacency that makes it easy to forget past sins of omission. But when the new pavements, which were the specific price of trolley privileges, begin to need extensive repairs and renewals, the old difficulties seem likely to reappear.[1] The

---

[1] Much of the pavement laid by the company does not meet the requirements of the specifications of the city, being of a less dura-

railway companies have no business interest in the maintenance of good pavements. Indeed, their business interests are distinctly opposed to them. The general use of the bicycle, a most formidable rival of the street cars in local transportation, is made practicable by smooth, well-kept pavements. In all large cities the bicycle has made serious inroads on the receipts of street railway companies, but in Philadelphia insult has been added to injury, since the irony of fate has compelled the companies to make smooth the highways of their adversaries. The induction from wide experience of corporate action in such matters, as well as the history we have just reviewed, seems to indicate that as the present pavement wears out the companies may be slow to recognize the need for repair and renewal.

The experience of Philadelphia emphasizes the generally recognized fact that a city should never entrust the care of its highways to any agent other than a municipal official or commission, so chosen as to be immediately and effectively influenced by public opinion. So long as public opinion, demanding well-kept streets, can only operate through a municipal officer who must be urged to the difficult task of moving a great corporation, often reluctant to act, and with large opportunities for delaying and even evading the discharge of duty, it will not be surprising if the streets are badly neglected.[1]

---

ble character than the city desired. The municipal officers stated that they found it inexpedient to attempt to enforce the specifications rigidly. The Chief of the Bureau of Highways in his report for 1895 reveals a somewhat remarkable system of inspection. He says: "Permit me to call attention to the fact that the Bureau is receiving the assistance of a number of inspectors assigned to duty upon the work of the passenger railway companies and other corporations, these inspectors being paid by the company or corporation whose work they are assigned to inspect. . . . In my judgment it is not calculated to produce the best results."

[1] It is interesting to note that in the report of the Bureau of Highways for 1896, Chief Hicks urges that the city should resume the responsibility of repaving and repairing all of its streets, and should arrange with the Traction Company for a percentage of gross receipts in return for release from the paving obligation.

II. *Tax on Dividends.*—A second form of obligation, imposed on most but not all of the companies, is the payment of a tax on dividends when such dividends are in excess of 6 per cent. Of the seventeen companies chartered before 1874, and maintaining their corporate existence until the recent consolidations, fifteen were obligated by their charters to pay the dividend tax, while two were exempt.[1] Of the fifteen some are obliged to pay 6 per cent. on the entire dividend, if it exceeds 6 per cent. on capital stock, while others are under contract to pay 6 per cent. on the excess of dividend above 6 per cent. on capital stock.

None of the companies chartered since 1874 have been required to pay a tax on dividends. There is no provision for it in the general incorporation law, and Councils have not chosen to exercise their right to impose the tax as a condition of their consent.

Although this obligation seemed unquestionable, the companies attempted to evade it. The *Sunday Dispatch* of October 9, 1859, calls the attention of the public to the fact that the dividend tax provision of the charters is not being enforced, and that no payments had been made except by the Frankford & Southwark Company.

The Controller's report for 1859 credits the Citizens Company with the payment of $253.50, presumably a dividend tax, although this is not specified. In 1860 two roads paid dividend taxes amounting to $2471.78. The following year the total return, three roads contributing, was only $1550.99.

In 1863 City Solicitor Brewster says in his report: "These (street railway) companies have hitherto been in the habit of deciding for themselves what amount should be paid to the city for dividend tax, and under their con-

---

[1] The two companies not specifically subjected to the dividend tax were the Lombard and South Sts. Co. and the People's Pass. Ry. Co. Their charters provide that the companies shall pay "such taxes and tolls as are now or may hereafter be imposed by Councils of said city, not exceeding in rate or amount that paid by any other railway company in said city."

struction of the law the receipts have been much less than they should have been. . . . Most of the railway companies have been making great profits and dividing among their stockholders very large dividends, amounting in many cases to fifteen and twenty per cent. on their investment."

The interpretation of the charter obligation to which the City Solicitor objected furnishes an excellent illustration of the devices to which the companies resorted to avoid the performance of their obligations. The amount of paid-in capital rarely reached the limit of the amount of stock which the companies were authorized to issue. In many cases the paid-in stock was not more than from 10 to 20 per cent. of the authorized capital. This fact suggested a means to avoid the dividend tax. The companies claimed that "capital" in the charter clause was to be interpreted as authorized capital, and began to pay on this basis. One of the companies, indeed, secured a supplementary act in 1864 construing capital as authorized capital.

The amount paid under this interpretation was very small, and a City Solicitor who was zealous in his care of the interests of the city, brought suit in 1865 to compel payment on a basis of paid-in capital. The case was framed against a company with a paid-in capital of $192,750 and an authorized capital of $500,000. The company contended that the payment should be on the basis of the latter amount. On appeal, the Supreme Court decided that "capital" in the charter meant paid-in capital.[1] Two cases involving this same point were brought before the Supreme Court in 1866, and the earlier decision was affirmed.[2] Thus by three successive decisions this question was settled.

But the resources of the railways for evasion of dividend taxation were not exhausted by these decisions. In 1883

---

[1] Citizens Pass. Ry. Co. vs. Phila., 49 Pa. State Reports, 251.

[2] Second & Third Sts. Pass. Ry. Co. vs. Phila., 51 Pa. State Reports, 465; Phila. vs. Gray's Ferry Pass. Ry. Co., 52 Pa. State Reports, 177.

a case appeared before the Supreme Court in which a new manifestation of legal ingenuity was given. The charter of the Ridge Av. Passenger Ry. Company provided that there should be paid "annually" into the city treasury "a tax of 6 per cent. upon so much of any dividend declared which may exceed 6 per cent. upon their said capital stock." The directors were authorized to declare dividends at such times as they deemed expedient. The Company maintained that their charter thus provided that if any single dividend exceeded 6 per cent. it became subject to taxation, but if, for instance, during the year quarterly dividends of 6 per cent. were declared, amounting to a total annual dividend of 24 per cent., the tax provision did not apply, since no single dividend exceeded 6 per cent. The Court was not impressed with the legal force of this argument, and the common sense interpretation of "annually" received a judicial sanction which defeated a most ingenious attempt to pervert the intention of the law.[1]

The result of the legal contest in 1865 and 1866 was the collection by the City Solicitor of more than $11,000 in 1865, and of about $46,300 in 1866, a large proportion of these amounts being arrears due. From that time collection seems to have been irregular for several years. From 1873 to 1878 the tax yielded from $21,000 to $25,000 annually. From that time it increased. In 1880 it was $36,548. In 1885 it reached high water mark of $104,043. The last return, that for 1895, gives as the amount collected for dividend tax, $92,339.20.

An investigation made in 1895 indicated that the companies were paying several thousand dollars a year less than conformity with the provisions of their charters requires. After giving figures of several companies, the writer concludes: "An examination of these figures seems to show that in the case of each of these roads the capital stock

---

[1] Phila. vs. Ridge Av. Pass. Ry. Co., 102 Pa. State Reports, 190.

issued, instead of the paid-in capital, is made the basis of ascertaining the excess upon which the company is liable."[1]

III. *Car License Fees.*—The third form of obligation to the city, and the one which has been enforced with the least difficulty, is the tax on cars, imposed upon all companies. The ordinance of 1857 exacted an annual license fee of five dollars on each car " intended to run." The car tax was increased in 1859 to $30 and in 1867 to $50, at which rate it has since remained. An additional tax of $50 is imposed on each car regularly operated on a line which crosses a bridge owned by the city. The amount yielded by this tax as reported by the City Controller is as follows for the years indicated:

1860	$10,173
1865	11,345
1870	24,058
1875	27,914
1880	40,191
1885	47,987
1890	54,209
1895	76,163
1896	97,550

Unfortunately, ease of collection is the only merit which the car tax possesses. It evidently tends to keep the number of cars provided by the company down to the lowest limit necessary to accommodate the traffic, and is thus responsible in some degree for the greatly overcrowded cars from which the city suffers.[2]

---

[1] Albert A. Bird—Phila. St. Railways and the Municipality. *Citizen*, January, 1896.

[2] In these days when loud complaint is made that the companies do not provide a sufficient number of cars, it is somewhat amusing to note that early in the history of the railways, when the validity of the car tax was questioned, it was sustained by the Court on the ground that it was a proper exercise of the police power as a means for limiting the number of cars and thus preventing obstruction of the highways.

We are now able to make a close approximation to the amount received annually by the city of Philadelphia in return for street railway franchises which the financiers of the Union Traction Company value at about $75,000,000. We have seen that the return to the city is of three kinds, the paving and maintenance of the streets, a dividend tax and a car tax. The amount of the dividend tax and the car tax is perfectly definite, and it is possible to make a close estimate of the value of the paving and maintenance obligation.

The estimate of the Bureau of Highways of the amount expended by the railways on repaving the streets is $9,000,000. The Union Traction Company claims to have expended $14,000,000. Taking the figure of the Bureau as a basis, we have as the approximate total return to the city from the special taxation of the street railway companies:

Paving and maintaining streets.......	$450,000 [1]
Dividend tax	92,000
Car tax	97,000
	$639,000

The amount which the city thus receives from its railway companies is equivalent to a tax of six per cent. on present gross receipts, and of about nine-tenths of one per cent. on the estimated value of the franchises.[2]

In addition to the municipal taxation described, the passenger railway companies are subject to taxation for State

---

[1] This amount is 5 per cent. interest on $9,000,000 expended on paving. It is understood that these pavements were laid under a ten year guarantee by the paving companies, who must maintain them during that time. Afterward the companies will be subject to a renewal charge, estimated at $450,000 annually by Mr. Thomas Dolan, a prominent director. An official of the Bureau of Highways states that the renewal estimate is excessive.

[2] This does not include taxes on real estate, which the companies pay in common with all real property holders. This tax amounts to about $45,000.

purposes. In common with all corporations, the companies pay a tax of one-half of one per cent. on the actual value of their capital stock, and in common with all transportation companies, they pay to the State eight-tenths of one per cent. of gross receipts.[1] This taxation yielded the following amount for the year ending November 30, 1896, as reported by the Auditor-General:

Tax on capital stock $432,844.17
Tax on gross receipts 91,391.85

Total State tax................$524,236.02

The total annual amount paid by the street railway companies of Philadelphia to city and State is thus at present about $1,163,000, inclusive of interest on investment in pavements and exclusive of ordinary taxation on real estate. This sum is equivalent to a tax of about eleven per cent. on gross receipts.

A few comparative figures of the rates of taxation paid by street railway systems elsewhere are of interest in this connection. It should not be forgotten, however, that conditions of railway service differ widely in different cities and such comparative figures should therefore be used with caution.

The terms on which the Toronto, Canada, railways are operated have been much discussed during the past few years as an object lesson for other cities. Toronto bought the roads, and in 1891 leased them to an operating corporation on the following terms. The railway company pays to the city an annual rent of $800 per mile of single track and a progressive percentage of gross receipts, beginning at 8 per cent. on receipts up to $1,000,000, and reaching a

---

[1] All bonds held by citizens of Pennsylvania are subject to a State tax of four-tenths of one per cent., but since this is a tax on the bondholder rather than on the company, the tax on bonds is not reckoned as an element in the special taxation of street railway companies.

maximum of 20 per cent. on all receipts above $3,000,000. Tickets are sold regularly at the rate of six for twenty-five cents; special workingmen's tickets, limited to the early morning and early evening, at eight for twenty-five cents, and school children's tickets at ten for twenty-five cents. If the Toronto system were applied to the railways of Philadelphia at the present time the annual net return to the city would be about $2,000,000, or about $800,000 more than is now received by both city and State. This estimate makes allowance for the fact that under the Toronto plan the cost of construction would be chargeable to the municipality, not to the companies as at present.

In Baltimore the railway companies are under obligation to pave between their tracks and twenty-four inches outside the outer rail, to pay a direct tax of two per cent. to the city on the market value of their stocks, in addition to a small tax on stocks to the State, and to pay 9 per cent. of gross receipts into the city treasury for the maintenance of the public parks. They also pay a very small car tax. These provisions applied to Philadelphia companies would insure the city a return of approximately $3,350,000, in addition to the paving between the tracks, the annual value of which cannot easily be accurately estimated. Thus the application of the Baltimore plan would nearly treble the present return to the public.

No other cities on this side of the Atlantic have in the past dealt as wisely with their railway franchises as those already mentioned. For instance, the consolidated Boston companies, under the West End Company, paid only $325,288 as taxes for the year ending September 30, 1895. In New York City the system of taxation is so complex that it is impossible to make a general comparison of any value. Under an act of 1892 all lines thereafter constructed pay a tax of 3 per cent. on gross receipts for the first five years, and thereafter 5 per cent. of gross receipts, and since 1893 all franchises have been publicly sold at auction under statutory requirement. New York thus seems likely to get a fair return for all future privileges, although little has been realized in the past. Chicago has likewise realized very little from its railway franchises.

An examination of the conditions on which other American cities have bestowed their railway franchises shows that Philadelphia has, on the whole, realized more than other large cities, with two notable exceptions. But looking toward the future, it seems probable that those cities in which the street railways hold franchises for comparatively brief periods will soon be in enjoyment of a larger proportional return, either in taxes or in lower fares, than Philadelphia can hope to receive, unless municipal ownership should prove practicable. For as the present franchises expire, these cities will be able to readjust their contracts in the light of the experience of Glasgow and of Toronto, while it will be exceedingly difficult for Philadelphia to materially alter the existing obligations of her companies.

CHAPTER VI.

PUBLIC CONTROL.

In order to understand the nature and limitations of the power of control possessed by the city of Philadelphia over her railway companies, it is necessary to glance at the circumstances under which the railways were chartered. The system began to develop at a period when the General Assembly of Pennsylvania was exercising its constitutional right to enact special and local legislation in a manner which resulted in much harm to local interests as well as grave demoralization of the legislature. Acting in a strictly local affair, without local knowledge or local responsibility, the State legislature granted the streets of Philadelphia to the railway companies on such terms as it saw fit. The conditions under which the companies obtained their privileges were thus prescribed by an authority which was not competent to deal wisely with the parties to the street railway contract, even if it had been disposed to deal fairly with them.

The antagonism of the interests of State and city first appears in the prodigality of grants to railway companies in face of strong opposition on the part of the citizens of Philadelphia to the excessive multiplication of the railways. The feeling of the city is expressed by a resolution of Councils, dated April 2, 1858, against the provision by the State legislature for the construction of additional lines of railway without consulting the municipal legislature. Councils furthermore requested that the General Assembly delegate to them the exclusive right to legislate in the matter of street railways. The answer to the protest was the grant of nine charters in April, 1858, and six additional charters in 1859.

These charters varied considerably in form, but almost all of them gave opportunity for the assertion of the city's right of regulation by requiring the consent of Councils for the construction of the roads, or, in some cases, by binding the companies to obey ordinances made for the regulation of street railway companies. However, in 1868, the General Assembly attempted to nullify the powers of control which had been earlier bestowed upon the city, by the passage of an act which was significantly styled by press and people the "Railway Boss Act."[1] This noteworthy bit of legislation provided "that the several passenger railway corporations in the city of Philadelphia shall pay annually to the said city, in the month of January, the sum of $50, as required by their charters, for each car intended to be run over their roads during the year, and they shall not be obliged to pay any larger sum; *and said city shall have no power by ordinance or otherwise to regulate passenger railway companies unless authorized so to do by the laws of this commonwealth, expressly in terms relating to passenger railway corporations in the city of Philadelphia;* provided, that nothing contained in this act shall be construed to release said companies from keeping in good repair the streets on which the rails are laid, and from paying to the city the additional cost of constructing sewers along the lines of their roads, under an act approved May eight, one thousand eight hundred and sixty-one."

The constitutionality of this act was called into question in a suit between the Union Passenger Railway Company and the city, on the ground that it impaired the obligation of contract created by the charter of the company, which fixed the license fee of each car at $30, but the Supreme Court of Pennsylvania refused to declare the act unconstitutional in this respect,[2] and this judgment was affirmed by the Supreme Court of the United States, to which the case was carried on appeal.

The act was again involved in a notable case arising

---

[1] Act of April 11, 1868.
[2] Union Pass. Ry. Co. vs. City of Philadelphia, 83 Pa. State Reports, 429.

through the attempt of the city to enforce the paving obligation against one of the companies, which claimed that under the act of 1868 its obligation was not to repave but only to repair the street.[1] In deciding the case in favor of the city the Supreme Court ignored the act. Its present force is thus left indeterminate.

As a curious example of the kind of regulation which the General Assembly undertook after the passage of the "Railway Boss Act," a statute of April 17, 1869, is interesting. This statute provides that "It shall not be lawful for any passenger railway company, or their officers, agents, employees or any other person or persons, to use salt on any passenger railway tracks or street within the corporate limits of Philadelphia," and then prescribes a penalty for the unlawful use of salt. And then two supplementary acts, one passed in 1870 and another in 1872, proceed to exempt from the prohibition certain portions of certain streets, declaring that within the specified boundaries the railway companies may salt their tracks at their discretion. The spectacle of the legislature of a great State gravely considering such a question as the establishment of metes and bounds within which the railways of Philadelphia shall be allowed to use salt to remove snow and ice from their tracks is happily made impossible at the present time.

The recognition of the evils of the domination of local interests by a body out of touch with local needs was one of the most potent factors in the movement which led to the adoption of a new State Constitution in 1873.[2] Art. III,

---

[1] Ridge Av. Pass. Ry. Co. vs. City of Philadelphia, 143 Pa. State Reports, 444.

[2] The spirit in which the Constitution was framed is judicially set forth in the following words: "It is part of the pervading intent of that instrument to give local bodies the control of local affairs. . . . One of the prime objections of the people in calling a constitutional convention was to do away with special legislation which interfered with local affairs or granted privileges to particular bodies and withheld them from others with a semblance of partiality rather than of equal favor to all." Allegheny City vs. Railway, 150 Pa. State Reports, 411.

section 7, of the present Constitution provides that no local or special legislation incorporating or granting privileges to railway corporations shall be passed, and with reference to street railway companies the Constitution says: " No street passenger railway shall be constructed within the limits of any city, borough or township without the consent of its local authorities."[1] Thus the era of usurpation by the State of local functions of control in street railway matters came to an end.

Returning now to the consideration of the power of control which was vested in Councils, we find that it is largely based upon provisions inserted in most of the early charters and in several of the later acts incorporating the companies, requiring the consent of the Councils before the railways could be constructed. The usual form of the provision was to the effect that the consent of Councils should be assumed unless disapproval was expressed within thirty days after the passage of the act.

In 1857 Councils had made an ordinance to regulate passenger railways, and when the requisite consent for the construction of lines was given, the railway companies were forced to file written agreements binding themselves " to observe and be subject to all ordinances of the city in relation to passenger railways then in force and thereafter to be passed." The companies were thus definitely committed to obedience to municipal regulation.

We have seen that not all the charters required the consent of Councils. In almost all of those that do not specify consent, however, the companies are expressly bound either to observe the ordinance of 1857 or to observe " all ordinances heretofore or hereafter to be passed." In only two charters is it expressly stated that the consent of Councils shall not be required. This was the case of the Empire Passenger Railway Company, chartered in 1869, and the Union Passenger Railway Company, chartered in 1864. The latter act was passed over the veto of the Governor by

---

[1] Constitution of Pennsylvania, Art. XVII, sect. 9.

the corrupt influence which was behind it, while the Empire Company was chartered under circumstances which suggest grave suspicion of corruption. These charters provide in terms which seem purposely ambiguous that the companies shall be subject to ordinances " regulating the running of passenger railway cars."

The right of control rested on the original charter and ordinance provisions until the companies asked Councils to give them the privilege of changing their motive power from horses to electricity. In 1876 the General Assembly had authorized passenger railways in cities of the first class[1] " to use other than animal power in the carriage of passengers in their cars, whenever authorized to do so by the Councils of said city."[2] Under this act two cable lines were constructed, one running east and west and the other north and south. The rest of the lines were operated by horses until 1892. Then the companies sought from Councils the privilege of using the overhead electric system of propulsion. The first ordinances granting this privilege on a few of the lines were passed in face of great public opposition on March 30, 1892, and imposed no new conditions on the companies. In response to an irresistible public demand for a *quid pro quo*, however, all the later ordinances bestowing these privileges on the rest of the lines imposed carefully specified obligations on the companies as a condition of the assent of Councils.

Thus the present power of control possessed by the city rests upon the original charter provisions, the original ordinances giving the requisite consent of Councils for the construction of the roads, and on the so-called " trolley ordinances " which reaffirm the obligation of the companies to obey all regulations made by ordinance.[3]

---

[1] For purposes of legislation, the cities of Pennsylvania are divided into three classes, by a law of May 8, 1889. All cities having 600,000 or more inhabitants belong to the first class. Philadelphia is the only city at present in this class.

[2] Act of May 8, 1876.

[3] For an enumeration of these regulations see pp. 81, 82.

Since the power of the city over the companies is thus, in the case of most of the companies, dependent largely on ordinance provisions imposed as a condition of consent to the exercise of privileges by the railway companies, it is important to determine the legal right of the city to maintain such regulations. The legality of conditions thus specifically imposed by Councils is upheld in a strong opinion by the Supreme Court handed down December 30, 1893. The opinion says: "The man who can give the whole can give part, or who can grant absolutely can grant with a reservation of rent or other condition. He who can consent or refuse without reason does not make his consent or his refusal either better or worse by a good or a bad reason. It is conceded that the local authorities may impose some conditions, such as those relative to the police power; but where is the grant to any other body to supervise and limit the conditions or say what they shall be? The Legislature clearly cannot do it. . . . Nor can the courts trespass upon the discretion given by the Constitution absolutely to the local bodies. . . . It would require a very clear case of contravention of some controlling and paramount principle of public policy to justify an interference by the courts to put a limit on the unlimited constitutional grant."[1] The case in which this opinion was rendered involved the legality of a provision by the city councils of Allegheny requiring the payment of a dividend tax and fixing the rate of fare, but the language of the Court is general in its application.

In the case just cited, the charter of the company involved had been granted after the adoption of the present State constitution, which expressly requires the consent of local authorities for the construction of street railways, and thus the circumstances of the grant were somewhat different from those under which most of the Philadelphia companies are operating, since the provision for the consent of Councils was simply legislative in their case, not constitutional. But fortunately the Supreme Court has rendered an opinion in

---

[1] Allegheny City vs. Railway, 150 Pa. State Reports, 411.

a similar case arising under a charter granted previous to 1874 and in which the provision for local consent did not rest on a constitutional mandate.

In this case,[1] dating back to 1870, the Supreme Court decided that under a special charter provision of a street railway company requiring the consent of the local authorities for the construction of the line, the city was justified in imposing a tax on cars and a tax on dividends as the conditions of its consent. The language of the decision is most explicit on the question of local control of the company. " The power of the municipal authority to give or refuse consent is unlimited and unqualified. That necessarily implies the power to impose reasonable conditions in giving their consent. If they impose unreasonable conditions, all the company can do is to refuse to accept."

It is thus definitely determined by the highest tribunal of the State that all conditions imposed by Councils in granting the consent made necessary by the provision of the special acts chartering the companies up to 1874 and by the constitutional provision since that time are valid parts of a contract entered into between the city and the railway companies.

The ordinances and some of the charters provide that the companies shall agree to observe the terms and conditions of all laws and ordinances then in force or thereafter to be passed relating to the government, control or regulation of railways within the city of Philadelphia. The scope of the regulation which may be exercised under this sweeping provision has never been judicially determined, but it would seem that the only limitation upon the authority of Councils is the requirement that the regulations imposed must be reasonable. The City Solicitor in a recent opinion takes this view.

Having considered the nature and the scope of the control which the city may exercise over its street railway com-

---

[1] Federal St. Ry. Co. vs. City of Allegheny, 14 Pittsburg, Leg. Jour., N. S., 259.

panies, we have now to learn what use the municipality has made of its authority up to the present time.

The first ordinance regulating street railways was that of July 7, 1857.[1] The provisions of this ordinance, briefly summarized, are as follows. The companies are required:

(1) To build their roads in accordance with plans approved by the city Board of Surveys and Regulations.

(2) To maintain, pave, repave and repair all streets occupied by their tracks.

(3) To make repairs or to pave streets on order of the Chief Commissioner of Highways, under penalty of a stoppage of their cars.

(4) To employ "careful, sober and prudent agents, conductors and drivers."

(5) To refrain from running their cars at a speed greater than six miles an hour in the "built-up portions of the city."

(6) To pay an annual license fee of five dollars "for each car intended to run."

(7) To file a statement of the entire cost of their roads and to concede to the city the right to purchase the same at any time.

The provisions requiring the companies to pave the streets and to pay a license for each car have already been considered at length, and the important provision allowing the city to purchase the roads at any time will receive separate and detailed consideration later.[2]

This original ordinance was slightly amended in 1859. The principal change was the insertion of a clause directing the Commissioner of Highways to pave streets which were neglected by the companies and to collect the cost through the law department.

No regulations of importance in addition to those of the ordinances of 1857 were made until 1876. In that year Councils decreed that the Lombard and South Streets Passenger Railway Company should be allowed to use a bridge

---

[1] See appendix, p. 117, for text of ordinance.
[2] Chapter VII, p. 83.

owned by the city on condition of a reduction of fare from six cents to five cents.[1] In 1881 it was ordered that no further privileges be granted to railway companies except on condition of five-cent fare.[2] It will be noted that Councils did not stand upon their right of regulation conveyed by the agreement of many of the companies to observe all ordinances "to be passed," but made the regulation part of the terms to be exacted when railway companies asked for further privileges.

This reduction of fare was evidently made in a somewhat abnormal mood of virtuous regard for the interests of the citizens as opposed to those of the railway companies, for we find Councils speedily relapsing into their ordinary condition of indulgence toward the railway interests. When opportunity came to apply their regulation in the case of two important companies they granted the privileges and expressly waived the condition.[3] Nevertheless, in a few instances they stood by their declared intention and brought about a reduction of fares under the ordinance of 1881.

No further extension of the city's function of control was attempted until the passage of the "trolley ordinances," beginning in 1892. These ordinances make the following provisions for the regulation of the companies accepting the franchise for the use of the overhead electric system:

(2) The companies must pave, repave and maintain in good order at all times the streets traversed.

(3) The companies must agree to observe all laws and ordinances which are in force or shall be made relative to passenger railway companies.

(4) Their construction and equipment must be subject to the approval of the Director of Public Works.

(5) They must remove the overhead electric construction whenever Councils by ordinance so direct.

---

[1] Ordinance of July 14, 1876.
[2] Ordinance of June 16, 1881.
[3] Ordinance of Feb. 9, 1884, and April 14, 1886.

(6) Cars shall be run at certain prescribed intervals.

(7) The rate of fare for a single continuous ride shall not exceed five cents from five o'clock A. M. to midnight, and shall not exceed ten cents from midnight to five o'clock A. M.

(8) The roads shall in no way conflict with the construction and maintenance of elevated roads.[1]

During the past year there has been much discussion of the possibility and the advisability of exercising the power of control to reduce fares, to shorten the hours of labor for the employees, and to provide vestibules for the protection of the motormen, but no action with reference to the regulation of these matters has been taken by Councils.

---

[1] See appendix for text of ordinance.

CHAPTER VII.

MUNICIPAL OWNERSHIP.

Within the past few years the question of the advisability of extending the functions of the State in the industrial field has been much debated in the United States. The European experiments with public ownership and management of railways, telegraphs, gas and electric plants, and street railways have been eagerly watched from this country, while the recent bolder ventures of certain cities, especially those of Great Britain, in the direction of "municipal socialism" have been followed with deep interest. The prevalent American faith in the doctrine of *laissez faire*, so effectually preached by the older economists, has weakened as the power of aggregated capital has increased through ever widening combination. Supported by European experience and by a few successful American experiments in municipal ownership of gas and electric lighting plants, and furthered by revelations of corruption in the grant of franchises and award of public contracts under monopoly influence, the arguments in favor of the municipalization of lighting, communication and transportation facilities have deeply impressed a large number of the influential business and professional men of our cities, while the wage-earners, represented by the labor organizations, are enthusiastic in their advocacy of municipal ownership of such public enterprises.

Under these conditions a consideration of the possibilities of municipal ownership of the street railways of Philadelphia is of much importance. The situation in Philadelphia in this respect is unique. In many cities railway franchises are granted to private corporations for a definite period. In some cases at the end of the period the municipality becomes the owner of the road.[1] In others the city has the right of purchase at the end of the franchise term.[2]

In the case of the Philadelphia railways the General Assembly has placed no limitation on the period of their corporate existence.[3] But it was provided that the charter privileges should not become operative until the city had given its consent to the construction of the lines. In giving the requisite consent the Councils prescribed certain conditions, among which was the following most important provision: " That the directors of any such company or companies shall, immediately after the completion of any passenger railroad in the city, file, in the office of the City Solicitor, a detailed statement, under the seal of the company, and certified under oath or affirmation by the president and secretary, of the entire cost of the same; *and the City of Philadelphia reserves the right at any time to purchase the same, by paying the original cost of said road or roads and cars at a fair valuation.* And any such company or companies refusing to consent to such purchase shall forfeit all

---

[1] Berlin, Hamburg and Cologne, in Germany, and Buda-Pest, in Hungary, become owners of their roads at the expiration of the franchise terms.

[2] All English cities can buy their railways twenty-one years after a charter is granted to a private corporation, paying the cost of replacing the roads at the time of purchase. Many cities in England have already bought their railways under this provision.

In Toronto, a railway company was granted in 1861 a franchise for thirty years, and at the end of that time the city bought the roads at a price fixed by three arbitrators appointed under an act of the Provincial Parliament.

In Cleveland, Ohio, the City Council determines the length of the franchise period under a statutory provision fixing a maximum term, which until the last session of the Legislature was twenty-five years, and is now fifty years in some special cases. The Council " may renew any such grant at its expiration upon such conditions as may be considered conducive to the public interest." Or the Council may refuse to renew the grant and purchase the road.

[3] In two cases the original charters limited the corporate existence to twenty years, but the limitation in each case was subsequently removed.

privileges, rights and immunities they may have acquired in the use or possession of any of the highways as aforesaid."[1]

This is certainly a remarkable provision in view of the fact that it was made at the beginning of the development of street railways and at a period when the doctrine of *laissez faire* held almost undisputed sway in the United States. Its adoption by the councilmen of 1857 gives evidence either of remarkable forethought which one would hardly predicate of Philadelphia Councils of that period, or of a lack of understanding of the significance of such a clause. The latter hypothesis seems the most reasonable. It is supported by the fact that little attention seems to have been given to this clause in the discussion which raged over the new system of transportation at the time.

The advantages of municipal ownership of the street railways were suggested by the Chief Engineer and Surveyor of Philadelphia in a report presented to Councils in 1855, and it seems probable that the important clause in the ordinance of 1857 was inserted as a result of his suggestion, without serious consideration of its far-reaching possibilities.

When the introduction of a street railway system was first under discussion, Mr. Strickland Kneass, the Chief Engineer, a man eminent in his profession and of wide influence, was requested by Councils to investigate the system and report to a special committee on city passenger railroads. Addressing the chairman of the committee, under the date of October 12, 1855, he "begs leave to offer a few remarks preparatory to your report to Councils," and proceeds to point out the great advantages of the proposed innovation over the existing omnibus system. After dwelling on the technical details of railway construction, he closes his communication with the following recommendation, which is certainly worthy of quotation in full: " As regards the policy that should govern the construction of city passenger railroads, I am inclined to the opinion that to secure

---

[1] Ordinance of July 7, 1857, Sect. VIII.

the true interests of the city, as well as their proper management, they should be built and maintained by the corporation—the city issuing a license for each car to companies who may have each the exclusive use of a certain route, the company to pay annually an amount that shall be an assessment upon each passenger carried, the rates to be regulated annually from sworn returns made by the officers of the company.

" The cars will then bear the same relation to the city that the omnibuses now do, and will prevent incessant clashing between companies that would otherwise be compelled to use a portion of each other's routes; it will place in the power of the city the means to correct abuses, preventing imposition upon its citizens and the creating what should be a public benefit, a nuisance. The city will then know where to look for the proper repair of its highways, and not be, in a measure, dependent upon a company of individuals whose only interest will be the amount of dividends realized.

" If it is advisable (and I agree such is the case) that a commencement be made at once, such contracts should be entered into with capitalists who seek the investment, as will enable the city to obtain the possession of the roads as soon as the financial condition of its treasury will permit, or whatever arrangement to reach that point Councils may decide upon."

The clear-sighted engineer who so accurately forecast the difficulties which the city later realized in dealing with the private companies should thus be given a large measure of credit for the unusual reservation of the power to purchase the roads at any time.

In later days the companies have declared that the purchase clause has no force, but it is apparent to any one who reviews the history of the time that the clause was clearly understood and definitely accepted by the original incorporators. Many citizens objected to the new railways on the ground that they promised enormous profits to the promoters and threatened dangerous monopolies. The railway incorporators, in published statements, replied that the argument was absurd, since the city could avail itself of the reserved right to purchase the roads at any time at the original cost if it was found that the new enterprise was yielding excessive profits.

The clause seems to have been ignored until very recent years. Only once was it used by the public as a threat to bring the companies to terms, and then it was ineffectual. When the fare was raised from five to six cents in 1864 the Common Council ordered the report of an ordinance to provide for the purchase of the roads charging the advanced fare. But no further action was taken.

The formation of the Union Traction Company in 1895 and its action in abolishing free transfers gave rise to a formidable agitation against the company and incidentally to a strong demand for the exercise of the reserved right of purchase. The existence of the clause conveying the right was unknown to most of the citizens of Philadelphia, and the newly discovered possibility of acquiring the lines was hailed with much enthusiasm. At a great mass-meeting held December 5, 1895, to protest against the action of the Union Traction Company in abolishing free transfers, every expression of the speakers in favor of municipal ownership was greeted with loud applause by an audience which was apparently rather conservative in character. The resolutions adopted by the meeting closed with the following paragraph:

"*Resolved finally*, That if the Union Traction Company shall fail to meet these just demands in such a spirit, the said committee shall be charged with the duty of considering whether the people should not assert their primary right and exercise their reserved power of purchasing the street railways, and with the further duty of addressing all candidates for Councils on this subject, and of leading a popular movement to support no candidate who will not pledge himself to sustain the rights of the people."

On January 9, 1896, the Municipal League presented to

the Common Council a resolution favoring municipal assumption of the lines, and a similar communication was received from the committee appointed by the mass-meeting just mentioned. This committee included some of Philadelphia's most prominent and influential citizens, ex-Governor Pattison, ex-Postmaster John Field, and Senator Penrose being leading members of the body. On the same day that these communications were received an ordinance providing for the purchase of two roads was introduced and referred to committee.

For a time it looked as if the movement for immediate municipal ownership would assume formidable proportions, but the Union Traction Company quietly pursued its announced policy, making no concessions to the demand for lower fares or restoration of transfer privileges, and the agitation gradually subsided. The public seem to have accepted the new conditions, and at the present moment (January, 1897) there is no public discussion of municipal ownership.

Meantime the question of the legal right of the city to secure the roads under the ordinance of 1857 is of the utmost importance to the citizens and the stockholders alike. The financial results of purchase on the terms of the ordinance would be startling. The clause gives the city the right to purchase at "the original cost of said roads." There is no allowance for the value of the franchise. Thus interpreting the clause literally, the city could buy the Frankford and Southwark Passenger Railway for about $1,800,000, the latest reported cost of construction and equipment, while at present market rates the stock of this company is worth about $12,525,000.

It seems incredible that the public and the railway investors alike should have ignored a provision which permits such radical financial reconstruction of the railway system at the pleasure of the city, but although in the absence of judicial interpretation of the purchase clause it is impossible to speak with certainty, there is much force in the argument that the ordinance provision is entirely valid and capable of putting the municipality into possession of at least a large part of the railways.

The case of the right of the city to purchase rests upon these facts: The charters under which almost all of the railway companies of Philadelphia operate required the consent of Councils for the construction of the roads. In giving the necessary consent, Councils required these companies to file a statement of cost of construction and an agreement to comply with the provisions of the ordinance of 1857, which contained the purchase clause, as a condition of their consent to the occupation by the companies of the streets of the city.[1] In addition, several of the companies were expressly made subject to the ordinance of 1857 by provisions in their charters. The others in accepting their franchises with the condition that they observe all ordinances made by the city for the regulation of passenger railway companies seem to have accepted the purchase clause. The Supreme Court of Pennsylvania, in decisions already cited, has upheld the right of a municipality to impose such conditions as it chooses in giving consent to the occupation of its streets by passenger railway companies.[2] Therefore the acceptance of the franchises on the express conditions of the ordinance seems to have made the purchase clause a valid part of the contract between the city and the railways. And furthermore, the recent "trolley ordinances" have specifically reaffirmed the obligations of the companies, save the few which obtained the trolley privileges on March 31, 1892, to accept as binding " the terms and conditions of all laws and ordinances now in force, or which may hereafter be passed relative to the government, control or regulation of railways."

---

[1] A recent search of the records has brought to light statements of cost of construction by five of the companies, all filed in 1859, in accordance with the requirement of the ordinance. The rest of the statements that were presumably filed cannot be found.

[2] See page 78.

With reference to the validity of the purchase provision, the Law Committee of the Municipal League, which made an investigation of the relations of the municipality and the railways a few years ago, said in their report: " So far as the researches of your committee have gone, no reason has been discovered why the city has not a legal right to take advantage of the provision referred to, and it would seem, if authority were needed to authorize the city to lease or operate railways so acquired, that it might be acquired from the acts of Assembly incorporating the several companies which by reference have incorporated the ordinance of 1857 as part of said acts."

During the recent agitation, the Law Committee of Councils sought an opinion from the City Solicitor with reference to the effect of the change of motive power on the validity of the purchasing clause. The Solicitor's opinion was naturally very guarded. He said: " How far, therefore, the right of the city to purchase, under the terms of the ordinance of 1857, may have been affected by the lapse of time, by changes in the companies and by the granting of new privileges, or whether the delay and granting of new privileges may be held to be a waiver by the city of the right to purchase, are questions which the court would be required to pass upon; or possibly a jury, if any question of fact arose. At the time of the filing of the statements the power to purchase undoubtedly existed, and still exists, unless affected by the facts I have referred to." In its report to Councils, the committee says truly: " It is a fact that Section 8 of the ordinance of 1857 has stood there unchallenged, unamended, unrepealed. As each road has been granted additional privileges by Councils, it has, by its own agreement, made itself amenable and liable to its provisions. It is an integral part of every grant to occupy a street for railway purposes. Every dollar that has been spent upon every railroad in Philadelphia has been spent with full knowledge of its existence. Changes in corporations have taken place, new companies have been formed under new laws, improved methods of transit adopted, new systems of pavement introduced; some of the companies have filed statements of cost as required by it, and all subject to this apparently plain, direct contract with the City of Philadelphia, that they should surrender all under the conditions of the section. A magic spell seems to have been over all for nearly forty years—railway managers and city officials alike—to have permitted so far-reaching and important an enactment to lie totally neglected and apparently forgotten."

In view of the large financial interest involved, it is apparent that when the interpretation of the clause is demanded from the courts the resources of legal subtlety will be exhausted in the attempt to secure a decision denying the right of purchase, or imposing terms that will make it impossible for the city to realize the advantages of lower fare.

CHAPTER VIII.

CORPORATE INFLUENCE IN STATE AND MUNICIPAL GOVERNMENT.

The people of the United States are sadly familiar with the fact that the relations of the representatives of the people and private corporations conducting enterprises depending on grants of public franchises have not in the past been marked by the maintenance on either side of high ideals of honesty and just dealing with the public. Men of strict integrity in private relations have as directors of corporations participated in actions which have made the term "corporate conscience" a byword among Americans. When the lecturer of the Ethical Society of Philadelphia announced during the agitation for lower fares that he would speak on "The Morals of the Union Traction Company," the town smiled and insisted that he had chosen a barren topic, for the Union Traction Company had no morals. Yet its high officials are without exception men whose business integrity in private dealings is beyond question. Whatever may be the basis for the feeling thus reflected, the general impression that great corporations enjoying public franchises consider themselves morally irresponsible is unquestionably a most serious factor in our present social situation.

It is often urged by those who deprecate the extension of governmental functions that public ownership and management of enterprises based on public franchises would result in lamentable corruption of our politics by increasing the number of places in the gift of successful politicians, thus adding strength to the motive which makes and maintains political machines for private aggrandisement. Whatever may be the force of this argument, it is unfortunately true that close beside the Scylla of public management there is a Charybdis of private control. In Philadelphia, as elsewhere, private corporations enjoying public privileges have found it desirable to corrupt government for their own ends, and have been most successful in realizing their desires.

The history of corporate corruption in the street railway field begins with the inception of the system. The right to build street railways in Philadelphia was given to each company by special act of the General Assembly. The General Assembly in those days was a body notoriously ready to exercise its power of special and local legislation in behalf of those who offered in return a consideration which was not expected to find its way into the public treasury. There is little doubt that some of the early charters were purchased. Apart from the specific charges of the newspapers of the day, one cannot review the numerous charters granted in 1858 and 1859, in face of the forcible protest of the best citizens of Philadelphia against the reckless multiplication of companies, without feeling assured that the grants were not prompted in every instance by considerations of public expediency alone.

But the most notorious instance of corruption came a little later in the open purchase of the charter of the Union Passenger Railway Company in 1864. It is beyond question that options on stock were liberally distributed among members of the General Assembly to secure this charter. When the act incorporating the company was passed, the *Sunday Dispatch* declared, not without truth, " There is nothing in the statute books which conceals a more nefarious and scandalous history than that which is connected with this last legislative atrocity."

The motives which led Councils to give the necessary consent for the construction of the lines are not beyond question in all cases, but it should be remembered that the local legislators attached conditions to their assent which probably seemed to them to insure ample compensation to the public for privileges bestowed. It is also to their credit that they entered formal protest against the grant of their streets by a body unfamiliar with local needs, and although they afterward gave their consent to the very charters against which they had protested, it may be urged in justification that they knew the General Assembly might grant these privileges a second time without requiring their consent, and so deemed it wise to improve the opportunity to secure a return to the public by a conditional approval.

Perhaps the most striking instance of the influence of the railway companies on the State legislature during this early period is the so-called " Railway Boss Act " of 1868, already alluded to,[1] which provided, first, that passenger railway corporations in the city of Philadelphia should pay $50 annual license fee for each car, and then proceeded, " and said city shall have no power, by ordinance or otherwise, to regulate passenger railway companies unless authorized to do so by the laws of this commonwealth, expressly in terms relating to passenger railway corporations in the city of Philadelphia."

This act, as generally understood, is an indication of the fact that the companies had a surer grip on the legislature of Pennsylvania than on the Councils of Philadelphia, and so attempted to secure themselves against interference from the city. If this interpretation is correct, their hold on the General Assembly was destined to be less useful to them than they anticipated in 1868, for six years later a new constitution forbidding local and special legislation was put in force by a people out of patience with the corruption and inefficiency encouraged by the former constitution, which gave practically unlimited scope to local and special legislation.

Meantime, while the government of the State was partly redeemed by the new constitution which limited the power of the General Assembly for evil, the government of the city had fallen into the hands of a band of political conspirators within the Republican party known as the Gas Ring.[2]

---

[1] See p. 74.

[2] See chapter on the Philadelphia Gas Ring in Bryce's American Commonwealth, Vol. II.

Building on their control of the gas department, they gradually incorporated into their structure of corrupt power almost every department of municipal government. The ownership of one of the principal street railways of the city aided their schemes by increasing the number of votes under their control. The main advantages to the railways of the Gas Ring regime were non-enforcement of their obligations to the city.

In 1881 a citizens' Committee of One Hundred broke the power of the Gas Ring, and in 1885 the reformers secured the passage of a new charter for the city of Philadelphia, under which much has been done during the past ten years to better the government of the city on the executive side. Little has been accomplished, however, in the way of securing better local legislators.

Although the influence of the companies in city and State had been exerted on occasion to further the plans of the railways at the expense of the public, as has been indicated, no systematic attempt to control public officials appears to have been made until within the past twelve years. But, just about the time that the city was shaking off the yoke of the Gas Ring, a new influence made itself felt in State and local politics. The Philadelphia Traction Company, chartered in 1883 with the purpose of consolidating and operating existing street railways, and representing a powerful aggregation of capital, soon came to wield an influence with which political leaders found it necessary to reckon.

Councils early yielded to the hypnotic spell of the Traction Company. In 1881 they had bravely enacted that no further privileges should be granted to street railway companies except on condition of reduction of fare to five cents.[1] In 1884[2] and in 1886[3] we find them granting additional privileges to the West Philadelphia Company and the Union Company and expressly waiving the requirements of five

---

[1] Ordinance, June 16, 1881. [2] Ordinance, February 9, 1884.
[3] Ordinance, April 14, 1886.

cent fare, and we note the significant fact that these companies were both leased and operated by the Philadelphia Traction Company.

But the influence of the Company was first clearly revealed to the public in 1887. In that year it rushed through the General Assembly a bill providing for the incorporation of motor companies and giving them extraordinary powers. The newspapers denounced the bill and the methods by which it had been forced through the General Assembly, and a great mass-meeting was held in Philadelphia on March 1, 1887, to enter protest against its approval by the Governor.

The methods of the Company and the character of the legislation which it had presumed to attempt are reflected by the speeches at the meeting and the editorials of the newspapers. Mr. W. W. Porter said at the mass-meeting: " This act, I say with deliberation, would reconstruct the corporation law of Philadelphia for the individual and selfish purposes of one corporation. . . . This bill would give a power of monopoly to throttle you and me and all of us." Mr. Hampton L. Carson, the distinguished historian of the Supreme Court, denounced the act as " an example of reckless and arbitrary power outgrowing all the bounds of decency and restraint." The conservative *Public Ledger* says of the bill: " It is wrong in policy, bad in principle, a trick and a fraud." And again the *Ledger* explains the public hostility to the company by saying that it is due to " the breaking of their bargains with the city, their pretence of abiding by the decisions of the courts of law, with their attempt to circumvent the courts by covered up and tricky proceedings in the legislature, and their defiant contempt of public rights."

The Traction Company bent before the storm. The bill was recalled by the General Assembly and again passed with some of its most objectionable features stricken out. But when the storm had passed, the Traction Company was still in possession of the field.

Soon the people of Philadelphia began to realize with increasing vividness that the public welfare was being subordinated in many instances to the interests of the railway corporations. The press freely and forcibly voiced the protest of the best element in the community against the domination of the corporations, but the railway interests were too strongly intrenched to be dislodged by the attacks of the newspapers. From the indignant citizen who asserted that "Traction owns the town" to the judicious editorial writer of the *Public Ledger* who spoke of "their defiant contempt of public rights," every Philadelphian felt that the railway companies were corrupting the municipality and controlling legislation for their selfish purposes.

A single instance, and that a recent one, will suffice to illustrate the extent of the political influence of the railway corporations. In the fall of 1894 the Philadelphia Traction Company attempted to obtain the right to use important streets in the northern district of Philadelphia. Under inspiration easily understood, Councils framed an ordinance giving to the Traction Company the exclusive right to the use of nearly one hundred miles of streets in one of the suburban districts, exacting absolutely no return for the exceedingly valuable privileges conveyed. The Traction Company did not even agree to build railways through the streets. It simply acquired monopoly right to hold the locations and use them if it wished.

Nothing but dense ignorance or corruption could have prompted such an ordinance at a time when every man who read the newspapers knew that in other cities similar privileges were eagerly sought by capitalists under conditions which secured large remuneration for the public. While the ordinance was pending the press exposed and denounced the scheme with unanimity and force. Councils were vehemently charged with corruption and threatened with popular vengeance. But the arguments of the Traction Company availed more with Councils than even an aroused public opinion. They passed the ordinance with large majorities. The mayor vetoed it, and although the Traction Company had commanded on the first passage more than the necessary three-fifths vote to carry the ordinance over the veto, the Company apparently determined to yield to a public opinion that was growing ominous, and the veto was sustained.

And now comes the most remarkable part of the story. Every newspaper of repute in the city regardless of party had denounced the "Suburban Trolley Grab," as it was termed, and now as the annual municipal election approached, at which one-half of the Common Councilmen and one-third of the Select Councilmen were to be chosen, they demanded the defeat of every man who had voted for the " Traction Grab Bill." Lists of those who voted for the bill were published in all the papers, and their respective parties were exhorted not to renominate them.

But the political machine responded to other forces than those of public opinion. The terms of seven select councilmen who voted for the bill expired. All but one were renominated and all nominated were re-elected. In the Common Council the terms of forty-seven supporters of the "Traction Grab" expired. Thirty-six were renominated and thirty-five re-elected. The net result of the agitation of a united press and a long and vigorous reform campaign in behalf of honorable candidates was the election of one reform councilman. A more remarkable assertion of the control of a municipality by a political machine identified with the interests of a railway company it would be hard to find.

The Philadelphia press, pulpit and platform have continually proclaimed in recent years, practically unchallenged, that a considerable number of councilmen are in the pay of the street railways and other great corporations. It is generally known that until recently the recommendation of a councilman was the surest road to an appointment to a position in the service of the Traction Company. The attempt to control the municipal legislature by corrupt influence was so open that no intelligent citizen could fail to see it. The railway companies are by no means responsible for all of the evil, for electric lighting, telephone, paving and other interests are involved, but the railways have played an important part in the process of corrupting the public servants for their selfish ends, and they must bear their share of responsibility.

It is generally believed that the present Union Traction Company has abandoned the policy of attempting to control Councils by manipulating the political machine, and Philadelphia is thus one step nearer the realization of the hope that Mr. Bryce expressed in her behalf after describing her imposing city hall,—that "the officials who reign in this municipal palace will be worthy of so superb a dwelling and of the city where the Declaration of Independence and the Federal Constitution first saw the light."

CHAPTER IX.

THE RAILWAYS AND THEIR EMPLOYEES.

Everywhere in the country street railway employees were, until ten years ago, a sadly overworked set of men. In Philadelphia, as elsewhere, each car regularly operated was manned by a driver and conductor, who remained on the car from the time it left the barn in the early morning until it had completed the day's run late at night. This meant a daily service of from fifteen to eighteen hours of continuous work with very brief respite for breakfast, dinner and supper. For this service the ordinary compensation, at the beginning of the history of railways in Philadelphia, was $2 for the conductor and from $1.50 to $1.75 for the driver. This rate of wages has remained practically unchanged from the beginning to the present time, save in the rise of the pay of the man on the front of the car to a level with that of his fellow worker on the rear.

The evils of excessive hours were recognized during the early days by the public as well as by the immediate sufferers under the system. In 1864 a coroner's jury in its report on a case of fatal injury by a street car said, "Nor should we expect vigilance and attention from employees worn out by seventeen hours of incessant labor. . . . The constant occurrence of passenger railway accidents demands from this jury an unequivocal condemnation of the companies who compel men to do work to which the bodily and mental frame is not usually equal." In July, 1868, the conductors and drivers held a public meeting to urge the necessity of shortening the hours, but the companies refused to alter their schedules. It was stated at this meeting that the men were then averaging $2 for an actual working day of 18 hours.

The agitation which developed from time to time for the

reduction of hours accomplished very little until 1886. At this time an investigation showed that the usual working day on the Philadelphia Traction system was seventeen hours, with $2 pay for the conductors and $1.75 for the drivers. A short time before, the men on this system had worked nearly nineteen hours a day, but as a conductor testified, "so many of us became sick owing to the strain of long hours and the rapid bolting of our food, and so many resigned or threatened to do so, that the Company had to revise the time table." The People's line worked their men about seventeen hours, paying both drivers and conductors $2 per day. On the Cumberland Street line the men were on duty eighteen hours. The minimum day for street railway men, revealed by the investigation, was fourteen hours. Insufficient time was allowed for meals, and very frequently, when the cars were delayed on the street and fell behind the schedule, the men were unable to leave their cars for meals, being obliged to snatch a hasty lunch while at work. A *Ledger* editorial spoke exact truth in saying, "The horses have shorter hours, more regular feeding time and better care than the men."

Wages slavery was hardly too strong a term to apply to such service wherein the whole energy of a man, physical and mental, was absorbed in earning his daily bread, while in many cases the reserve force was drawn upon so heavily day by day that utter exhaustion speedily resulted. Normal family life was impossible for the street railway men working under these conditions. "When I want to see my children," said a conductor, "I have to see them in bed. I am off in the morning before they are awake and they are asleep when I come home at night. If they want to see me in the daytime they have to wait for my car."

In 1886 a wave of labor agitation swept over the country. The wage earners, under the leadership of the Knights of Labor, united in a general movement for shorter hours, higher wages and better conditions of labor. Thorough organization lent effectiveness to their demands. At this time the Knights of Labor, which had been in existence from 1869, grew in numbers and influence with remarkable rapidity. In 1885 it reported a national membership of 110,000. In 1886 it claimed 729,000 members. The strikes in the country, as reported by the National Bureau of Labor, increased from 645 in 1885, involving 2284 establishments and 242,705 employees, to 1411 in 1886, involving 9861 establishments and 499,489 employees.

The overworked street railway men throughout the country eagerly grasped the opportunity afforded by the general agitation to secure a more normal working day. In New York, Baltimore and other cities the men demanded ten and twelve hour days, and in several instances went on strike to enforce their demand. In Philadelphia the employees organized under the Knights of Labor and a local order, The Quaker City Protective Association, and then, with commendable moderation, they presented their case to the railway companies and to the public.

The companies resisted the movement for shorter hours until it became evident that public opinion was so thoroughly in sympathy with the very reasonable demands of the men that further resistance would be dangerous. At the beginning of the agitation several men had been discharged for taking part in the organization of the employees, but the organizers persisted, employing secret methods, and very shortly 3000 men stood ready to go on strike at the word of command. Then, on March 23, 1886, the Board of Arbitration on the part of the employees met the Board of Railway Presidents and presented their demands. They asked for the following concessions: (1) A working day of twelve hours; (2) Standard pay of $2 per day; (3) Relief from the necessity of buying uniforms, except a cap and badge; (4) The abrogation of the rule requiring drivers and conductors to clean their harness and cars; (5) An allowance of thirty minutes for dinner and fifteen minutes each for breakfast and supper; (6) The reinstatement of the men discharged for taking part in the agitation.

The Board of Presidents asked for a week to consider the matter. On April 1 another meeting was held, and after further conference the demands of the men were granted substantially as originally formulated. Thus the men obtained a reduction of hours without decrease of pay, and indeed with actual increase in some cases. They were also relieved from some of the petty exactions which had vexed them, and they obtained full recognition of their right to organize. The final negotiations were conducted in an admirable spirit of conciliation by both sides, and thus what threatened for some time to be a bitter conflict ended happily. The reduction of the barbarously excessive hours of street railway employees obtained in many other cities as well as in Philadelphia was one of the best results of the great labor movement of 1886.

During the succeeding session of the General Assembly the men attempted to render more secure the results of their victory of 1886 by obtaining the passage of an act making it unlawful for any officer of a passenger railway company to permit any person in the employ of the company "to work more than twelve hours of any one day in the service of said company; . . . provided, that all necessary labor over and above the time set by this section shall be considered overwork, for which the laborer shall receive additional compensation."[1] It will be readily seen on consideration that the act fails to afford the protection which was desired, for the proviso allowing "necessary labor over and above the time set by this section" practically nullifies the restriction which the act was intended to impose.

The employees of the Philadelphia companies rested content with the twelve hour day won in 1886 until the introduction of the trolley system and the consolidation of the companies altered conditions materially. The new system imposed much heavier responsibilities and harder work upon both of the employees who man a car. The serious

---

[1] Act of March 24, 1887.

results of the nervous strain upon a motorman of a rapidly moving electric car in city streets have attracted much attention from medical men, who tell us that the work on the front platform of a motor car develops a specific nervous disease. The conductor's burden is also increased by the change from the slow-going horse car to a rapid transit system, for in a given time he must handle a greatly increased number of passengers. Increase of responsibility and more arduous work naturally call for compensation in reduction of hours.

But reduction of hours did not occur in Philadelphia on the introduction of the trolley system, and as soon as the men began to feel the strain of the new work they grew restless. They began to organize. The movement attracted the attention of their employers, and in October, 1894, the employees of the Philadelphia Traction Company were warned that if they took part in a movement for organization they would be discharged. In January, 1895, President Mahon of the Amalgamated Association of Street Railway Employees of America, came to Philadelphia to promote the organization of the railway men under the Association. Soon after President Mahon's visit the local officers of the Association claimed a membership of 2000, out of a total number of about 6000 employees of the local companies. It was generally known that the men were much dissatisfied with the conditions under which they worked, and rumors of a strike were soon in the air.

In the fall of 1895 the railway companies of the city were consolidated under the Union Traction Company. Very soon after the organization of this Company the new management took two very important steps. They abolished free transfers, which had been used by about forty per cent. of the riders, and they declared war on the Amalgamated Association by discharging men who had been active in promoting the organization. The first discharges were made in October when twenty-two men were dismissed. The reason for the discharges was stated without reserve in notices signed by the General Manager and posted in the car houses, one of the notices reading:

Conductor John Douglass is hereby discharged for pretending to take an interest in his work with the company, and yet secretly exerting his influence and taking an active interest in the affairs of the Amalgamated Association of Street Railway Employees.

J. R. BEETEM,
General Manager.

The discharges had the effect of driving the men to more secret methods in the propaganda for the organization, and of precipitating their action.

October 20 a letter signed by the local officers of the Amalgamated Association was sent to the President and General Manager of the Traction Company, requesting the Company to consider the possibility of revising the schedules so that ten hours should constitute a day's work, the work to be performed within eleven consecutive hours, and the compensation to be not less than $2 per day.[1] An investigation made by the Toynbee Society soon after this time showed that although the men were nominally on duty twelve hours they were actually employed from thirteen to fourteen hours per day in many cases.

---

[1] In urging this consideration the men said: "The introduction of electricity for street car propulsion has brought with it greater responsibilities, labor of a more exacting and exhausting nature, and a mental and a nervous strain of such a character that the hours now fixed by law are too long to insure faithful and efficient performance of duty by the employees. We recognize this fact fully, and desiring to render the best possible service to you, our employers, beg leave to suggest the means by which we can be enabled to do so. There can be no disputing the beneficial effects of well requited toil. It is an incentive to a greater care of the company's various interests and property. By reason of shorter hours and less exacting labor we would be better able to prevent accidents and the destruction of limb, life, and property of our citizens who use the streets in the conduct of their business or as a thoroughfare.

The effect of shorter hours on the health and physical welfare of your employees will amply repay you for the small increase in outlay, if any. The return will come to you ten-fold in better work, a more careful guarding of the Company's interests, and, consequently, less damage to your property and that of the public."

This request of the employees for consideration was ignored, the General Manager declaring that the Company would not in any way recognize the Amalgamated Association.

It was very soon after these occurrences that the city was aroused to violent protest by the abolition of free transfers. The feeling against the Company was intense. A great town meeting was held December 5, in which many of the most influential citizens of Philadelphia participated. The press was almost a unit in denouncing the new policy, and in warning the Company that it was treading on dangerous ground in thus increasing the cost of transportation service to the people in face of the fact that the profits on actually invested capital were already enormous.[1] The wrath of the patrons of the Company and the condemnation of the press afforded a favorable opportunity for the presentation of the claims of the employees, which they were quick to recognize. An attempt was made to present to the mass-meeting the grievances of the employees, but the managers of the meeting declined to combine the issues of lower fare and shorter hours for the men. However, during the agitation

---

[1] The *Philadelphia Press* expressed a very general opinion when it said editorially with reference to the withdrawal of free transfers, "Undoubtedly some increase of revenue will be made, and, in the next few months, while stock is being worked off, much will be made of this. When the year is over this increase will be seen to be small. It will come high. Every penny of it will have estranged the public and embittered the city. Every passenger who finds his customary fare increased will cherish the wrong. Every jury will lay on damages a little heavier. Every voter at every chance will vote against the Union Traction. When paving repairs come up, future mayors will find an enthusiastic city behind them as they pile the burden on the Traction Company. *When strikes come, public opinion will favor the strikers.* Every fault in the Union Traction management will be magnified. The numerous benefits conferred by it will be utterly forgotten. . . . War is costly. The Union Traction has chosen war. Peace would be more profitable in the long run, and if the company is wise it will early retrace its steps. If it does not, a dozen years hence it will be struggling with a three cent fare, new paving outlays, and a hostile city."

over the fare question, the men made every effort in their power to get the management to consider the propositions formulated by the Amalgamated Association, and also to present their claims to the public. The Traction Company adhered to their original refusal to recognize the Association, announcing that they would listen to the grievances of employees who came to them as employees simply, but would have no dealings whatever with any organization representing the men. Meantime many men were discharged, and the employees claimed that most of them were dismissed simply because they had been reported as members of the Amalgamated Association. The policy of discharge to check the growth of the Association was a signal failure, serving only to weld the men together more closely. The organization flourished under the repressive measures attempted, and when, on December 14, President Mahon arrived to assume command, he claimed that he wielded an organization of 4500 men.

On the advent of Mr. Mahon, President Welsh, of the Traction Company, was again asked to consider the grievances as presented by the Association. No reply was made to the communication. A meeting of the employees was held on December 16, and another communication was sent to President Welsh, proposing that the entire matter in dispute be referred to an arbitration committee of disinterested citizens, " said Board of Arbitration to be composed of five men, two to be chosen by your Company, two to be chosen by our Association, and the four thus chosen to select the fifth man of said Board, and the entire matter to be submitted to this Board and their decision to be final." No reply was made to this proposition, the Company taking the position that there was nothing to arbitrate.

A strike was now seen to be imminent, and ex-Governor Pattison and Mr. Thomas Martindale were delegated by the Citizens Committee, that was attempting to secure a restoration of free transfers, to go before the Arbitration Committee of the Association and counsel the men against radical action. The representatives of the Citizens Committee found the men in session considering the advisability of an immediate strike. They attempted to avert the threatened action, but their mediation failed, and at midnight President Mahon, having received the requisite authority from the National Executive Board, issued an order to inaugurate a strike at 4 o'clock the following morning, Tuesday, December 17. With the parting injunction from the President, "Keep away from the rum shops, keep cool and let there be nothing like rioting," a memorable meeting was adjourned and one of the most serious conflicts between capital and labor which Philadelphia has ever seen was begun.

The men promptly responded to the strike order. On Tuesday morning the Company succeeded in moving a few cars, each one heavily guarded by the police, but before noon rioting began and many cars were abandoned on the street. Long before nightfall there was a complete tie-up. The employees of the single independent line, the Hestonville, Mantua & Fairmount Company, were not involved, and this road ran uninterruptedly during the strike.

The suspension of street railway traffic in a great city is a serious matter to the public under any circumstances, but in this case the situation was peculiarly unfortunate, since the paralysis of local traffic occurred just on the eve of the holiday season when the street railway travel is ordinarily at its maximum. But great as were the annoyances and the losses incident to the suspension of travel, the public generally accepted the situation with surprising good nature. The men had reckoned largely upon popular support, arguing that the almost universal hostility to the Company, which had resulted from the abolition of free transfers and the fear of further exactions from the recently organized monopoly management, would range the people of Philadelphia on the side of the employees in the coming contest. The public responded as the men had hoped. They cheerfully walked "for conscience sake," as a popular clergyman advised them to do. They rode contentedly in antiquated omnibuses, which in the emergency reappeared on streets that had not known them for forty years, or even in uncovered express wagons with empty boxes for seats.

Even the rioting did not alienate the sympathy of the people so largely as might have been expected. The Amalgamated Association had ordered its men to keep off the streets, and when attacks on the cars began, offered to detail men to guard the property of the Company, and a large proportion of the public credited the repeated assurance of the strikers that they had no hand in the riots.

On the second day of the strike a very few cars were run under police protection. There were occasional outbreaks of violence, but they were easily suppressed by the police, who were omnipresent and most effectively handled. Meantime several organizations and individuals were striving to bring about a conference between the men and the Company in order to arrange for arbitration, but the Company refused to listen to such proposals. "We have nothing to arbitrate," they said.

The third day found the situation little changed, save in the fact that the Company was evidently succeeding in securing men to operate their cars and would apparently soon be able to resume regular schedules if assured of protection.

On the fourth day the Company sent out a largely increased number of cars. In many instances the appearance of the cars under the control of imported men provoked attack from sympathizers of the employees, and the situation became more dangerous than on the earlier days, since the men on strike were growing desperate as the Company made progress in opening its lines. Thus it was with unspeakable relief that the citizens read the headlines in the papers of Saturday morning announcing that the strike was settled. Shortly before midnight on Friday, representatives of the Christian League had borne to the men a proposition, which they said came officially from the Company, declaring "if the men come back and return to their work and peace is restored, the Union Traction management will cordially and considerately receive any committee from the ranks of their own employees and will respectfully and kindly hear their complaints and grievances that they may offer, and will remedy the same within the range of fairness." After some hesitation the proposition was accepted by the men, and the strike was declared off.

But the rejoicing was brief, for when the men reported for duty Saturday morning they were met by an announcement from President Welsh that the Company was under obligation to keep a thousand men that had taken the places of the strikers, and therefore could take back at once only 3500 of the 4500 men who had gone on strike. The gentlemen who had acted in good faith for the Traction Company in negotiating a settlement had labored under a misunderstanding. The men refused to go back unless all were reinstated, and thus early on Saturday morning the strike was again declared on.

For three days more the people of Philadelphia were denied transportation privileges and were kept in constant apprehension of violence. Then on Monday night, December 23, after seven days of contest, the Traction Company and their employees came to terms. The strikers gained a recognition of their right of organization and a consideration of their grievances, but the company declined to discharge the men taken on during the strike, and, moreover, sustained their position of refusal to treat with the Amalgamated Association, the final agreement being made with a committee purporting to represent the employees of the Union Traction Company simply. The agreement on the part of the Company was as follows:

"1. We do not propose to govern the membership or connection of any employee with any lawful association; but such connection with such association of any character whatever must not enter into the relations between employees and the company, and cannot be recognized in the business conducted between us.

"2. That any grievance of whatever character that any man or men may have will always be considered fairly and promptly before such men and the officers of the company, and the company will afford such men an opportunity to examine the records of such employees to their entire satisfaction.

"3. We accept your statement that all men discharged since December 10, 1895 (except those discharged for just cause), will be reinstated upon examination of the records of such employees. The committee representing the employees to furnish the list of names of those they believe to have been unjustly discharged; and the men allowed to divide the runs, other than the runs laid out for the present employees, meaning those who have entered our services since the evening of December 17."

This agreement was brought about by the earnest efforts of disinterested citizens, Mr. John Wanamaker being the most prominent man in the later negotiations.

The result of the conflict was variously interpreted. *The Inquirer*, a paper friendly to the men, declared, "the Company has virtually surrendered," while the *Evening Telegraph* quoted the famous saying of the redoubtable John Phoenix, "I held the enemy down with my nose firmly fixed between his teeth," as expressing the situation with reference to the claim of the employees that they had won the fight.

But the trouble was not yet at an end. Within a few days the men charged the Company with bad faith, and claimed that the agreement of December 23 was being violated in spirit if not in letter. Meantime the employees had been seriously weakened by quarrels among their leaders. On Friday, January 3, a second strike was ordered. The strike was declared by President Mahon to be without due authorization, and in consequence few of the men responded. The strike was over by noon and the cars were running on schedule time.

The failure of the second attempt to strike, and the resulting disorganization, increased the dissatisfaction. The men grew more and more restless. They charged that the Company was discriminating against the old men by giving them the least desirable runs, and, moreover, that many of those who were prominent in the strike were being discharged without cause. In addition, they claimed that the Company was obliging the new men to sign an agreement to refrain from joining a labor organization. They also complained that they saw little prospect of achieving the reduction of hours for which they had engaged in the original strike. Relations became more and more strained, until by the middle of January it looked as if the men were about to go on strike again. A Committee of Six was finally appointed with instructions to secure definite assurance of redress of grievances or to order a strike.

Recognizing that the situation was serious, some of Philadelphia's best citizens intervened. Largely through the efforts of the Universal Peace Union, a Citizens Committee was appointed and a conference arranged with the officials of the Union Traction Company. It was then agreed that a Board of Conference should be created to consider the difficulties between the Company and the men. The Board was constituted of six representatives of the Union Traction Company, six representatives of the employees and six disinterested citizens. The six citizens were Archbishop Ryan of the Roman Catholic Church, Bishop Whitaker of the Episcopal Church, Bishop Foss of the Methodist Church, George Griffiths, Secretary of the Christian League, John E. Baird and John Sparhawk, Jr. The Board organized on January 16, and proceeded to a full consideration of the controversy. The employees were ready to agree to make the Board a court of arbitration and to bind themselves to accept the decision, but the Company refused to accede to this proposition. Thus the Board sat simply as a council of conciliation. The employees asked the Board to approve the following demands of the men:

1. Reinstatement of all employees discharged without just cause since December 10, 1895.
2. Restoration of old employees to their former runs.
3. A ten hour day with a daily wage of not less than $2.
4. The unquestioned right of organization.
5. Readjustment of pay of employees on sweepers, snow ploughs and of " trippers."
6. Receipt to conductors for money deposited each day, to avoid disputes over shortages.

The officials of the Company stated their case, and then the citizen section of the tripartite commission was entrusted with the duty of making recommendations. On Saturday, January 18, the citizens section submitted their report. They recommended the reinstatement of the men discharged because of membership in labor organizations, and future non-interference with labor organizations on the part of the Company. They begged the "generous consideration" of the Company for the request of the men for a ten hour day, but declared themselves incompetent to make a specific recommendation on this main issue of the contest. They further declared that they considered protection for motormen by vestibules as "absolutely essential," and welcomed the assurance of the Company that experiments were in progress to determine the best method of protecting the motormen on the front of the cars.

The officials of the Company agreed most cordially to accept the recommendations of the Commission and promised to do all in their power to carry out the suggestions offered. The men also assented to the terms of settlement, and so, after a month of conflict, peace was restored.

At the present moment the schedules have been revised so that only in a few instances do the working hours exceed twelve, while in many cases they are a few minutes less than that time. The pay is at the rate of $16\frac{2}{3}$ cents per hour for regular runs, and ranges from about $1.80 to $2.15, although the pay for "trippers" is, in some cases, as low as $1.15 per day. Vestibules have not been provided for the motormen.

The men are far from satisfied with their condition. They feel that the strain of the twelve hour service is a great hardship and are bitterly disappointed at their failure to secure the coveted ten hour day. Moreover, they have certain minor grievances, such as the lack of protection to motormen during the winter. But they seem to feel, on the whole, that there is no immediate possibility of remedying the evils of which they complain. They are utterly disorganized at present and unwilling to reorganize. They say that under present conditions an organization could accomplish nothing, since a strike would be hopeless with so many unemployed men to take their places. In an appeal recently issued they call attention to the hardships of long hours in the cold, and, asserting their own helplessness, beg the assistance of the public in securing a ten hour day and the enclosure of the front platforms.

There is a very general feeling in the community that the present working day is too long for the wellbeing of the men and for the safety of the public, and it is possible that Councils may be moved to exercise their power of control to reduce the hours. Such action would seem to be a very reasonable exercise of the police power, since the lives and property of citizens are unquestionably endangered by allowing an overworked motorman to run a car through crowded city streets.

BIBLIOGRAPHY.

The following bibliography has been confined to strictly local material in order that it might not be unduly extended.

Acts of Assembly, from 1857 to 1874. For special acts of incorporation.

Brightley's Purdon's Digest of the Statute Law of the State of Pennsylvania. For general acts of incorporation and statutes governing street railways.

Ordinances of the City of Philadelphia from 1857 to 1897. For municipal regulations.

Journals of the Select and Common Councils.

Pennsylvania State Reports, Philadelphia Reports and Weekly Notes of Cases. For court reports.

Opinions of the City Solicitor. Published with the ordinances since 1887.

Reports of the Auditor-General of Pennsylvania. Until 1874 these reports contained detailed statements of the financial condition and the equipment of the street railways of the State. Since 1874 the reports have simply given the amount of State taxation of railway companies.

Reports of the Secretary of Internal Affairs. Since 1874 these documents have contained the reports of the companies formerly published by the Auditor-General. For the past thirteen years the published statements have been so meagre that they are of little value.

Annual Messages of the Mayors of Philadelphia. The executive reports of the city accompany the messages. Of especial value are the reports of the Controller, giving the annual income from dividend taxes and car licenses, the reports of the Bureau of Highways, dealing with the paving obligation of the companies, and the reports of the City Solicitor with reference to the litigation of the city and the companies.

Street Passenger Railways of the City of Philadelphia—Report of the Committee on Law to Councils, April 2, 1896. A valuable report containing a comprehensive opinion of the City Solicitor on the right of the city to control the railways, accompanied by detailed statements of the legal obligations imposed on each company. Also contains the important laws and ordinances governing the railways.

Street Railway Supplement of the Commercial and Financial Chronicle, of New York. Most valuable for financial statistics.

American Street Railway Investments. Published as an annual supplement of the American Street Railway Journal.

Pennsylvania Securities. An annual guide for investors, dealing largely with local securities. Began publication as the Philadelphia Securities in 1890. Devotes considerable space to street railways, and contains some important summaries.

Finance and Commerce. A weekly financial journal published by the Pennsylvania Securities Co.

Reports of the Citizens Municipal Association. Published annually since 1887. A section of each of the reports is devoted to the consideration of the obligations of the companies to the city, and the lack of enforcement by the municipal authorities. Especially full on the paving question.

Municipal League Tract, No. 1. The City of Philadelphia; its Stockholders and Directors. By Charles Richardson. March, 1893. 15 pp. A discussion of the railways in relation to the city, showing that the profits of the companies have been very large, that, nevertheless, they have neglected their obligations, and proposing a campaign for better Councils to guard the public interest.

Watson's Annals of Philadelphia. Vol. III, p. 488. A few notes on the early history of the railways.

Scharf & Westcott. History of Philadelphia. 1884. Vol. III, pp. 2220-2205. Gives a very brief sketch of the history of street railways in Philadelphia, apparently as a background for biographies of prominent railway organizers.

Easton. A Practical Treatise on Street or Horse-Power Railways. Philadelphia, 1859. 140 pp. An interesting view of street railways at the very beginning of their development.

Report of the Committee Appointed to Secure the Colored People in Philadelphia the Right to the Use of the Street Cars. May, 1867. 8 pp.

Why Colored People in Philadelphia are Excluded from the Street Cars. Published anonymously, in 1866. 29 pp.

The Trolley System. Stenographic Report of Testimony of Experts and Arguments of Messrs. Shapley and Johnson. Allen, Lane & Scott, 1892. 138 pp. Presents the arguments in favor of the trolley system.

Objections to Overhead Electric Systems. 1892. An argument in opposition to the introduction of the trolley system. 24 pp.

The Overhead Electric Trolley Ordinances. Addresses in Opposition to their Passage. March, 1892. 82 pp.

Toynbee Society of Philadelphia, Pamphlet No. 1. The Philadelphia Trolley Companies and their Employees. December, 1895. 18 pp.

Files of the newspapers. The foregoing bibliography shows that the special literature of local street railway questions is very meagre. There has been much discussion of the financial and political aspects of the railways during the past ten years, but this discussion has taken permanent literary form only in the newspapers. Thus the files of the newspapers become a most important source for such a study as the present.

APPENDIX.

I. ORDINANCE OF 1857.—II. FORM OF RECENT ORDINANCES GRANTING TROLLEY PRIVILEGES.—III. STREET RAILWAY ACCIDENTS.

I. Ordinance of 1857.

Section 1. The Select and Common Councils of the city of Philadelphia do ordain that all passenger railroad companies within the city of Philadelphia shall be subject to the restrictions, limitations, terms and conditions hereinafter provided; and any such company, before entering upon any road, street, avenue or alley within the limits of said city, shall be understood and deemed to be subject thereto, upon the conditions hereinafter prescribed.

Sect. 2. (Makes certain technical requirements with reference to grades, style of rail, etc.)

Sect. 3. That all railroad companies, as aforesaid, shall be at the entire cost and expense of maintaining, paving, repairing and repaving that may be necessary upon any road, street, avenue or alley occupied by them. That for the convenience of the public it shall also be the duty of such companies to clear the streets, or other public highways that they may occupy, of snow or any obstructions placed therein by such companies, when the same impedes the travel upon said highways, and for any neglect on their part to do so for a period of five days, they shall be punishable by a fine of twenty dollars for each square that may be so impeded, recoverable before any alderman of the city of Philadelphia, and payable into the city treasury, upon a complaint of five citizens residing therein, upon oath or affirmation: provided, nevertheless, that whenever any such company shall deem it expedient to use their said road during the continuance of the snow they shall provide comfortable sleighs, or other suitable vehicles, for the transportation of passengers along the route of their railway at the usual rates as aforesaid; then, and in that case, no such penalty shall be recoverable.

Sect. 4. That it shall be the duty of any company, as aforesaid, when requested so to do by the Chief Commissioner of Highways to remove any obstruction, mend or repair their road, pave or repave the highways, as hereinbefore provided, and should they refuse or neglect to do so for ten days from the date of such notice, then and in such case the Councils may forbid the running of any car or cars upon the said road until the same is fully complied with; and the city reserves the right in all such cases to repair or repave such streets, and the expense thereof shall be a judgment upon the road, stock and effects of such company, recoverable as judgments are now recoverable by the city of Philadelphia.

Sect. 5. It shall be the duty of said company or companies to employ careful, sober and prudent agents, conductors and drivers to take charge of their car or cars when upon the road, and for the violation of any act of Assembly, or ordinance of the city, on the part of any such officer or officers, or employees upon said road, the company shall be liable to all fines, forfeitures or damages therefrom; provided, however, that this act shall not be taken to excuse or free any such officer or employee from the penalties or responsibilities of any such violations, or other acts by them committed.

Sect. 6. (An unimportant provision regulating the running speed of the cars and requiring notice of approach of cars.)

Sect. 7. It shall be incumbent on all railroad companies, as aforesaid, before placing cars upon their road, to pay into the office of the Chief Commissioner of Highways, and annually thereafter, for the use of the city, the sum of five dollars for each car intended to run on the same. They shall also have the number painted in some conspicuous place upon each car; and any omission or neglect to comply with either of these provisions shall be punishable by a fine of ten dollars, to be recovered on complaint before any alderman of the city, who shall pay the same forthwith into the city treasury.

Sect. 8. The directors of any such company or companies shall immediately after the completion of any passenger railroad in the city, file, in the office of the City Solicitor, a detailed statement, under the seal of the company, and certified under oath or affirmation by the president or secretary, of the entire cost of the same; and the city of Philadelphia reserves the right any time to purchase the same, by paying the original cost of said road or roads and cars at a fair valuation. And any such company or companies refusing to consent to such purchase shall thereby forfeit all privileges, rights and immunities they may have acquired in the use or possession of any of the highways as aforesaid. . . . .

Sect. 9. Any passenger railroad company which is now or may hereafter be incorporated in the city of Philadelphia, shall, by their proper officer or officers, who shall sign the same, file in the office of the City Solicitor a written obligation to comply with the provisions of this ordinance: provided, that no railroad company now incorporated shall be authorized to commence work upon any of the highways of the city until this section shall be complied with; and any failure to do so for ten days shall be taken and deemed as a refusal on the part of such company; and in case the Philadelphia and Delaware River Railroad Company should fail to comply with the provisions of this section on or before the eighth of July, proximo, the City Councils hereby express their disapproval of an act, entitled " A Supplement to an Act to incorporate the Philadelphia and Delaware River Railroad Company," approved June 9, 1857, which provides for the construction of a passenger railway, by a private corporation, over Fifth and Sixth streets, in the city of Philadelphia.

II. FORM OF RECENT ORDINANCES GRANTING TROLLEY PRIVILEGES.

Section 1. The Select and Common Councils of the city of Philadelphia do ordain, that permission is hereby granted to the .... Passenger Railway Company to occupy the following streets and to use electric motors as the propelling power of the cars on the tracks of said Company which are hereby authorized to be laid as follows: ....
....

Sect. 2. Said motors to be supplied from over-head wires, supported by iron poles, not less than twenty feet high, which the said company is authorized to erect and maintain, and to be placed opposite each other within the curb lines, and connected with the street wires, or at the option of the company to be erected in the middle of the street with a double bracket thereon suspending the overhead construction. The same to be of the kind, style and system as that now constructed by the Catherine and Bainbridge Streets Railway Company, and all feed wires shall be buried.

Sect. 3. Before any permits shall be issued by the departments of the city of Philadelphia to proceed with the work of constructing the railway and trolley system authorized by this ordinance, the said railway company shall enter into an agreement or contract with the Mayor of the city (who is hereby authorized to execute the same on behalf of the city), which agreement or contract shall be in form approved by the City Solicitor, and shall among other things provide: That the said railway company shall agree to keep and maintain in good order at all times, whether paved, macadamized or unimproved, all streets, avenues or roads traversed by its lines of railways, or by its trolley system; that the said railway company shall agree to accept as binding upon it the terms and conditions of all laws and ordinances now in force, or which may hereafter be passed, relating to the government, control or regulation of railways or railroads of any kind within the city of Philadelphia. That in the construction and equipment of its roadbed, cars and its trolley system, all kinds and character of materials, supplies or workmanship, plans, profiles, elevations, designs, etc., shall be subject in every way at all times to the approval and inspection of the Departments of Public Works and Public Safety. That the said company shall take down and remove the overhead trolley system whenever directed to do so by ordinance of Councils; that the said railway company shall run cars over their entire line at intervals not exceeding five minutes between the hours of 6 and 9 A. M. and 5 and 8 P. M., and at intervals not exceeding ten minutes at all other hours of the day, excepting between the hours of 12 midnight and 5 A. M., when they shall run at least every hour. The rate of fare to be charged for a single continuous ride over the entire line shall not exceed five cents; that the railway or trolley system herein authorized shall be so built and erected as not to interfere with the building or erecting and operating of an elevated railway or railroad on any of the streets or avenues herein named; that work upon the said railway or trolley system shall be begun within ten months, completed and in operation over the entire route herein named within three years, and that said railway company shall furnish and execute a bond in the form approved by the City Solicitor, and with security approved by the Mayor, in the sum of twenty-five thousand (25,000) dollars, conditioned upon the faithful execution and carrying out of all the terms and conditions of this ordinance and the agreement or contract herein authorized, which bond is forfeited to the city, and the money shall be paid into the city treasury if the said railway company shall default in its agreement.

Sect. 4. That the said company shall, under the supervision of the Department of Public Works, repave in good, substantial and workmanlike manner, with Belgian blocks, or other improved pavement, as directed by ordinance of Councils or by the Director of the Department of Public Works, and to be done in a manner to be prescribed by and to the satisfaction of the said Department, all streets to be occupied by it not already paved with such improved pavement, and also all other streets heretofore repaved with an improved pavement, the repaving of which is not satisfactory to the said Department, said repaving to be done from curb to curb for such length of street as shall be occupied by poles and trolley wires, or by other electric motive power system. Such repaving shall be commenced upon each of the said streets as soon as the construction of the roadbed or of the poles or trolley wires, or other electric motive power system shall be commenced thereon, and shall be pushed and completed with all reasonable and proper diligence as rapidly as such system is being constructed in said streets, or as Councils may by ordinance otherwise direct; if not thus pushed, the Director of the Department of Public Works may enter upon the streets and complete the same at the expense and cost of the said railway, trolley or other electric motive power company constructed therein; and that said company shall at all times hereafter keep the said paving in good repair when directed to do so by the Department of Public Works, so long as the said trolley or other electric motive power system shall be maintained on such streets: *Provided,* that such repaving or repairing aforesaid shall not free the said company from any other paving, repaving and repairing the streets occupied by it that may be required by any ordinance of Councils that has been passed, or from any other duty or obligation resting upon it regarding paving and repairing that is incumbent upon it under and in virtue of any act of Assembly; and that fifty dollars shall be paid into the city treasury by said company for the printing of this ordinance.

III. STREET RAILWAY ACCIDENTS.

The following table gives the total number of accidents caused by street railways from 1861 to 1884 inclusive, the totals being given for five year periods. The figures are taken from the reports of the companies to the Auditor-General and the Secretary of Internal Affairs. The table ends at 1884 because the figures for several years after that time are incomplete. The Philadelphia Traction lines made no report from 1885 to 1891.

	Killed.	Injured.	Annual average of fatal accidents.
1861-1864	29	44	5.8
1865-1869	50	87	10.0
1869-1874	56	80	11.2
1874-1879	38	97	7.6
1879-1884	59	171	11.8

The increase of accidents caused by the introduction of the trolley system in 1892 appears in the following table. The statement of fatal accidents is from the records of the Coroner's office and is reliable. The statement of cases of injury is from the reports of the Secretary of Internal Affairs, and is probably only partial.

	Killed.		Injured.
1891	18	1891-92	210
1892	31	1892-93	197
1893	35	1893-94	243
1894	67	1894-95	379
1895	65		
1896	66		

www.ingramcontent.com/pod-product-compliance
Lightning Source LLC
Chambersburg PA
CBHW031349160426
43196CB00007B/790